Vaiṣṇava Contribution to Varanasi

Vaiṣṇava Contribution to Varanasi

Editors

R.C. Sharma

Pranati Ghosal

Jñāna-Pravāha
Centre for Cultural Studies and Research
Varanasi

D.K. Printworld (P) Ltd.
New Delhi

Cataloging in Publication Data — DK
[Courtesy: D.K. Agencies (P) Ltd. <docinfo@dkagencies.com>]

Vaiṣṇava contribution to Varanasi / edited
by R.C. Sharma, Pranati Ghosal.
x, 166 p. 23 cm.
Contributed articles.
Includes passages in Sanskrit (roman)
Includes bibliographical references (p.)
Includes index.
ISBN 8124603421

1. Vaishnavism — India — Varanasi — History.
2. Art, Hindu — India — Varanasi. I. Sharma,
R.C., 1936- II. Ghosal, Pranati, 1956-.

DDC 294.551 209 542 21

ISBN 81-246-0342-1
First Published in India in 2006

Published by:
Jñāna Pravāha
Centre for Cultural Studies and Research
South of Samne Ghat, Varanasi - 221 005
Phones : (0542) 236 6326; *Fax* : (0542) 236 6971
E-mail: jpvns@satyam.net.in
Web: www.jnanapravaha.org

and

D.K. Printworld (P) Ltd.
Regd. office : *"Sri Kunj,"* F-52, Bali Nagar,
New Delhi - 110 015
Phones : (011) 2545-3975; 2546-6019; *Fax* : (011) 2546-5926
E-mail: dkprintworld@vsnl.net
Web: www.dkprintworld.com

printed by: D.K. Printworld (P) Ltd., New Delhi.

Preface

To serve Indian culture and express esteem to knowledge-endowed, prestigious Kāśī, were the main inspiring elements in the background of the foundation of *Jñāna-Pravāha*. Therefore, a well knit chain of programmes covering education, research and sacraments (*saṁskāras*); weaved "Radiance of Kāśī," as an annual performance.

Flow of knowledge is a perennial tradition in Kāśī, genesis of which transcends research and is unconstrained by the limits of religious as well as sectarian enclosures. Different principles and beliefs have taken birth here and have developed to their fullness. Like *mārgācalavyatikarākuliteva sindhuḥ*, this stream of knowledge is flowing uninterrupted even today with its energetic velocity. Following the change of seasons its nature has certainly under-gone some variations but the flow continues. *Jñāna-Pravāha* is a drop in this current of knowledge, which is astonishingly radiating Kāśī's enchanting treasure of encyclopaedic knowledge.

Seated in the centre, Śiva Himself manifest in different forms -- sometimes as Śaiva and sometimes Bauddha, sometimes Jaina, sometimes Śākta and sometimes yet another. The conception of *naviśvamūr-teravadhāryate vapuḥ* is true but a desire to experience His knowledge and acts (*līlā*) is also our end. Vaiṣṇava nature (character) of Kāśī or the Vaiṣṇava contribution to Kāśī is a link of the same chain of thinking. We are grateful to those erudite scholars who had participated in the two-day symposium held on 1-2 August,

2001 and presented their academic oblations through deliberation.

The majority of papers presented in the seminar were in Hindi but this volume gives their English version.

Smt. Bimla Poddar, Founder & Managing Trustee, Jñāna-Pravāha and Sri S.K. Mittal of D.K. Printworld. deserve special thanks for taking initiative in this publication. The assistance of Dr. Neeraj Kumar Pandey and Sri Chandraneel Sharma is also appreciated.

R.C. Sharma
Pranati Ghosal

Contents

List of Illustrations

Key to Transliteration

VOWELS

अ *a*	आ *ā*	इ *i*	ई *ī*	उ *u*	ऊ *ū*
(but)	(palm)	(it)	(beet)	(put)	(pool)
ऋ *ṛ*	ए *e*	ऐ *ai*	ओ *o*	औ *au*	
(rhythm)	(play)	(air)	(toe)	(loud)	

CONSONANTS

Guttural	क *ka*	ख* *kha*	ग *ga*	घ *gha*	ङ *ṅa*
	(skate)	(blockhead)	(gate)	(ghost)	(sing)
Palatal	च *ca*	छ* *cha*	ज *ja*	झ *jha*	ञ *ña*
	(chunk)	(catch him)	(john)	(hedgehog)	(bunch)
Cerebral	ट *ṭa*	ठ* *ṭha*	ड *ḍa*	ढ* *ḍha*	ण* *ṇa*
	(start)	(anthill)	(dart)	(godhead)	(under)
Dental	त *ta*	थ *tha*	द *da*	ध* *dha*	न *na*
	(path)	(thunder)	(that)	(breathe)	(numb)
Labial	प *pa*	फ* *pha*	ब *ba*	भ *bha*	म *ma*
	(spin)	(philosophy)	(bin)	(abhor)	(much)
Semi-	य *ya*	र *ra*	ल *la*	व *va*	
vowel	(young)	(drama)	(luck)	(vile)	
Sibilants	श *śa*	ष *ṣa*	स *sa*	ह *ha*	
	(shove)	(bushel)	(so)	(hum)	
Others	क्ष *kṣa*	त्र *tra*	ज्ञ *jña*	ळ* *ḷ*	ॠ* *ṝ*
		(*kṣatriya*)	(*triśūla*)	(*jñānī*)	(*play*)

अं (ं) *ṁ anusvāra* (nasalisation of preceding vowel) like *saṁskṛti*

अः *visarga* = *ḥ* (aspiration of preceding vowel) like (*prātaḥ*)

ऽ *Avagraha* consonant #'consonant (like:- *ime 'vasthitā*)

Anusvāra at the end of a line is presented by m (म्) and not ṁ

HINDI LETTERS (extras)

ँ = *ñ*	ं = ṅ	ड़ = *ṛa*	ढ़ = *ṛha*
(*candrabindu*)	(*anusvāra*)		

* No exact English equivalents for these letters.

KEYNOTE ADDRESS

1

Vaiṣṇava Contribution to Kāśī
An Introduction

Vidyanivasa Misra

THOUGH it has been held that the Vaiṣṇava and Śaiva are two opposite currents, this is not true. There is a famous *śloka* in Sanskrit:

> *ubhayayo rekhā prakṛtipratyayato bhinnavadbhavati* ।
> *kalayati kaścana gūḍho harihara vedaṁ vinā śāstram* ॥
>
> It is only he who does not have the knowledge of Śāstras sees difference between Hari and Hara.

In fact, both have the same nature and same character. Both have originated from one Substance. They differ only because of suffix. Suffix *i* is used in the word Hari and *a* in Hara. In fact, there is no other difference between Hari and Hara and this difference cannot stand in Kāśī, because the river Gaṅgā flows through Kāśī. Viṣṇu is the source of Gaṅgā and Śiva holds Gaṅgā on his head. Hence, when Gaṅgā is present here, a difference cannot occur between Śiva and Viṣṇu. The *Nārada Purāṇa* mentions that Viṣṇu is the body of Kāśī and Śiva dwells in it. The entire Kāśī is in the spirit of Viṣṇu. Then why Kāśī should not be accepted as a Vaiṣṇava pilgrimage? A place is accepted as a pilgrimage for five elements — river, mountain, ascetics and great personalities living there, and for shrines (*devālayas*), adoration and worship. According to the *Kāśī Khaṇḍa* there were 105 images of Nārāyaṇa here. Besides, there were images of Mādhava and different *avatāras*, temples and shrines as well. There were some Vaiṣṇava pilgrimages and some Śaiva pilgrimages too. The presence of holy men in Kāśī is already known and it will be later mentioned in detail that there has been a tradition of ascetics also, from the very beginning in Kāśī. More particularly, this tradition began with Svāmī Rāmānanda in the Middle Age was of different kind. Probably the *āśrama* (abode) of Svāmī Rāmānanda Ācārya was established here even before it. Perhaps the *āśrama* of Nimbārkācārya had also been established or there might had been some *maṭha* (residence of a devotee and his disciples). *Maṭha* of Keśaveśvara might had been established. But the Vaiṣṇava sect which began with Svāmī Rāmānanda has some speciality. He addressed the people directly.

Its credit also goes to two other great personalities, namely, Svāmī Rāmānanda and Mahāprabhu Śrī Vallabhācārya. The latter had come from the Tailang region and it is because of him that the Braja literature became so widespread and extensively popular. The disciples in the tradition of Svāmī Rāmānanda belong to far-off places as far as Maharashtra. They had composed their literary works in Hindi, which was developing as a language of common people. Both of them had their influence on people from Assam to Gujarat and also in south India. Books in Braja language were composed at Tanjavur and Tiruvananthapuram in south India in about nineteenth century. Credit goes to both the great personalities for enhancing and thereby making a literary language the language of devotion. It was a new current of Bhakti movement. This current has not only abolished the differences, but also created such a temperament which has awakened a belief and devotion among the common people that they also have the right to attain the proximity of God. They also may feel and realise God like a literate or a person of a good family, or may feel a rich person. Such possibility was revealed in the poetry of that age and these poetry were motivated by the great ascetics of that time. The contribution of Kāśī is already known to us. Sadguru Kabīra and saints like Ravidāsa were in Kāśī. Even in the later times this pure Vaiṣṇava tradition remained in vogue and uninterrupted in Kāśī. To consider it otherwise would be misleading.

When you come to the level of eulogizing the name, when you come to the level of determining an *ācārya*, the question arises as to how a saint, an *ācārya*, should be ? There is no difference among holy men, no matter whether he is Sūradāsa, Tulasīdāsa or Kabīradāsa.

The great virtues — others' well-being, sharing with others' distress or a particular type of internal and external purity, softness of heart — were common among them. Both of them have similar temperament. This temperament of Vaiṣṇava was developed in Kāśī at the level of philosophy and in the form of art as well as adoration. The two famous places — Ādikeśava and Bindumādhava — have been mentioned in the *Matsya Purāṇa*. In the next several scriptures the place Bindumādhava has not been mentioned. Some of the historians are of the opinion that Bindumādhava was added later. Bindumādhava has been mentioned by Tulasīdāsa. The *Matsya Purāṇa* has been considered very old. It has mentioned Bindumādhava, Bindutīrtha near Pañcagaṅgā, and Ādikeśava pilgrimage centre which was situated at the confluence of the rivers Varuṇā and Ganges. These references prove that Kāśī has a long tradition. The people who hold that Kāśī was not significant in early times and also in Vedic periods have no knowledge or understanding (judgement) of history. Since literature does not mention every incident of history, as such history written on its basis cannot be complete. History, which was composed on several fabricated conceptions, has proved false. The conceptions like all this land was non-Aryan's and regarding the extent of the limits of Āryan's land have all been proved false. The whole country has a history in its entirety, which cannot be understood unless there is continuity of tradition. Once we understand this continuity it becomes clear that the devotion to both Śiva and Viṣṇu and their different appearances (forms, shapes), had simultaneously been in vogue like the two essential supplements. Literature furnishes several evidences. The literature dedicated to Viṣṇu has been composed more in numbers than the Śaiva literature. A leading Sanskrit poet Madhusūdana Sarasvatī was contemporary to Tulasīdāsa and he had composed the *Ānanda Vṛndāvana.* He mentioned in it that he wants to have the concept of the unmanifested (unknown) Brahmā, but a fickle blue light comes in front of him and he becomes helpless. His famous *śloka* is as under —

> *vaṁśī-vibhūṣita-karānnavanīradābhāt*
> *pītāmbarādaruṇabimbaphalādharoṣṭhād* ।
> *pūrṇendusundaramukhādaravindanetrāt*
> *kṛṣṇāt paraṁ kimapi tattvamahaṁ na jāne* ॥

His evidences refuted those *paṇḍitas* to whom Tulasīdāsa's *Rāmacaritamānasa*, composed in Avadhī, appreared trifle. He said—

> *ānandakānanehyasmin jaṅgamastulasī taruḥ* ।
> *kavitā mañjarī yasya rāmabhramarabhūṣitā* ॥

He has also composed the *Bhakti Rasāyana,* which analyses *bhakti rasa* in the *Śrīmadbhāgavata*, and a *kāvya* named *Ānanda Kādambinī.* On the other hand, he had composed the scripture *Advaita Siddhi*, which speaks of non-dualism (Advaita *mata*). Earlier he was monistic, but later got influenced by Caitanya Mahāprabhu and as such became his disciple. He had composed a commentary on the *Gīta-Govinda.* That is the first commentary from the viewpoint of spirituality. He was a resident of Kāśī. After him there has been an uninterrupted tradition of ascetics and worshippers, which has been in vogue till our contemporary venerable Svāmī Karapātrī Jī. He has composed the *Vedārtha Pārijāta* and made commentaries on several significant scriptures. He has written on Marxism and Rāmarājya, while on the other hand, he has made an interesting appreciation of devotion. The people used to get engrossed in such analysis or showed keen interest whenever he made an explanation on the exposition of *rāsalīlā* of *Śrīmad Bhāgavata*.

The tradition of such temperament of *Bhāgavata*, as to say Vaiṣṇava, has been uninterrupted in Kāśī. It has never been restrictive to the adoration of Śiva in any way. Had it been so then how could the image of Bhagavān Viṣṇu be placed in the temple of Bhagavān Viśvanātha? Although the image is not present here now, its space can still be seen. The process of salvation does not complete without bowing to it. There is a tradition in vogue that if a person visits Bhagavān Viśvanātha he has to reverentially murmur Rāma at least eleven times. Worship of Viśvanātha Jī is not complete without repeating the name of Rāma. These holy legends and traditions establish that Kāśī has always emphasized a convention of harmony. Such controversy would have been elsewhere.

I do not mean to say that there has not been any controversy, any cracking of heads everywhere, but at least Kāśī has escaped it. Kāśī has been a place for the people of all sects, regions and for all the regional traditions. Kāśī has truely been a city where people are holding their regional integrity. Those who have come here — about four hundred years ago, are living peacefully. They have come from Maharashtra, Gujarat, Lahore, but they all have accepted Benaras. They have shared and are sharing the language, conduct and views and festivals of Kāśī physically and wholeheartedly. Such may not be the situation in any other city. People from different state or culture have their own associations, councils, organizations, schools, etc., yet we find a co-ordination among them.

They play drama on the occasion of Gaṇeśa Caturthī. The drama is played not only in Marathi, but in Hindi too. There are people belonging to the Gauḍīya sect. They present their programmes in Bengali as well as in Hindi. What does it mean? We do not know the reason behind this spirit that linked them with Kāśī. Viṣṇu is present in each body and perhaps this is the actual reason. Or may be the holy Gaṅgā which flows in Kāśī does not make any difference, is the reason; or the reason is the amity between Śiva and Viṣṇu which had been seen in the marriage procession on the occasion of Pārvatī's marriage: Śiva is seen sitting as a bridegroom. Since He could not bow or bless everyone, He bows his head to Brahmā as He is the oldest god. Śiva blessed all *devatā*s by gesture only once. But he gave an amiable smile to Bhagavān Viṣṇu. Bhagavān Viṣṇu also responds with a brief smile. It means that both of them have a deep affection and understanding for each other. Tulasīdāsa has also mentioned the same exposition in the *Rāmacaritamānasa*. He has laid that as much as Śiva understands Viṣṇu, Rāma understands Śambhu, Sītā understands Pārvatī, and as much as Pārvatī as a questioner could understand Sītā, none else could understand.

We should never forget this point. A person often in excessive enthusiasm begins to think as to who is dominant, Śiva or Viṣṇu? So we should not become over-enthusiastic; rather we should keep in mind that Kāśī has the prestige of being a prominent land; it has the grandeur of sky that is full of knowledge and the currents of Gaṅgā flowing down through it.

These situations are sufficient for which the people of Kāśī may justifiably feel proud of it. But at the same time a great responsibility to upkeep this tradition comes upon them. This Kāśī should not get out of hand in which the whole of the universe seems to be arranged in harmony, and in which Śiva and Viṣṇu appear to be bound in love. This harmony should not be lost in any case.

PRESIDENTIAL ADDRESS

2

Vaiṣṇava Contribution to Radiance of Kāśī

Goswami Shyam Manohar Ji Maharaj

WHAT is the texture of Vaiṣṇava sect in Kāśī and how this sect has contributed and in which form to Kāśī? In fact, Kāśī is that city which has been a stronghold of not only Vaisnavism but also of all the sects, beliefs, doctrines, traditions, arts of India. Nothing exists isolated from it, be it music or poetry or something else, nothing is without any relation to Kāśī. Beginning from Ācārya Śaṅkara to Ācārya Vallabha, the whole chain is interwoven. The difference between Śiva and Viṣṇu, as presented by people, is in reality not a difference. If we think deeply, we will find that in fact the river Gaṅgā is the current of devotion. *Śrīmad Bhāgavata* mentions clearly —

> *madguṇaśrutimātreṇa mayi sarvaguhāśaye* ।
> *manogatiravicchinnā, yathā gaṅgāmbhaso'mbudhau* ॥
> *lakṣaṇaṁ bhaktiyogasya nirguṇasya hyudāhṛtam* ।
>
> — *Bhāgavata*, 3.29.11-12

This is a distinguishing feature of *nirguṇa bhaktiyoga* (inculcating devotion to the Ultimate Being viewed as unqualified). Just as the current of the Gaṅgā is flowing uninterrupted, in the same manner the current of devotion (*bhakti*) is also flowing all over India. When this holy river was brought down from heaven, then who assumed it? Except Bhagavān Śaṅkara nobody could've been able to assume it. So he had to assume it. He was prayed to assume it, initially he held the tremendous current in his matted hair, and then let loose one of this locks, which acted as a source of this present holy current for us, it is then that we had obtained this current. What I mean is that from Ācārya Śaṅkara there were five prominent schools namely, Kevalādvaita, Viśiṣṭādvaita, Dvaita, Dvaitādvaita and Śuddhādvaita. Several doctrines developing separate meanings and distinct sects developed from the separate branches of these very same *ācāryas*, and came into vogue. But what I mean prominently is that in *Śrīmad Bhāgavata* we get a summary of all the Vedas and Śāstras. Veda is prime, no object has any existence without Veda. We can enjoy the taste of fruits while seeds have no taste. It is contained only in fruits.

gāyatrī bījam vedo vṛkṣaḥ and *śrīmadbhāgavatam phalam* ।

It means that Gāyatrī is the seed, Veda a tree, and *Śrīmad Bhāgavata* is like a fruit.

Therefore, it is said in the beginning —

nigamakalpatarorgalitaṁ phalaṁ śukamukhādamṛta-drava saṁyutam ।
pibata bhāgavataṁ rasamālayaṁ muhuraho rasikāḥ bhuvi bhāvukāḥ ॥

— *Bhāgavata* 1.1.3

Both the words are mentioned here. Neither only passionate (*rasika*) is mentioned here nor only sentimental (*bhāvuka*). Both are mentioned here: *rasikāḥ* and *bhāvukāḥ*. A man should be aesthete (*rasika*) as well as imaginative (*bhāvuka*). If we hold both of them, then only we can enjoy the essence of *Śrīmad Bhāgavata*. We attain full perfection in the savour of *Śrīmad Bhāgavata*. When we speak of Bhagavān Śaṅkara, then we notice that in the *rāsalīlā* of Bhagavān Kṛṣṇa there has always been place for Bhagavān Śaṅkara. Even today one can see a temple of Gopīśvara Mahādeva at the site of *rāsa* which is called Vanśīvaṭa in Vṛndāvana. That is not different from that place. We attain that delight when we immerse in that savour. There is a mention of Madhusūdana Sarasvatī. He was an erudite scholar of Kevalādvaita. His book *Advaita Siddhi* is an authentic work of Kevalādvaita school. We cannot find any authority more reliable than it, and on the other hand the same Madhusūdana Sarasvatī composed the scripture *Bhakti Rasāyana* —

> *navarasamilitaṁ vā kevalaṁ vā pumartham* ।
> *paramamiha mukunde bhaktiyogaṁ vadanti* ॥

Madhusūdana Sarasvatī mentioned its first *maṅgalācaraṇa* as under —

> *navarasamilitaṁ vā kevalaṁ vā pumartham* ।
> *paramamiha mukunde bhaktiyogaṁ vadanti* ॥
> *nirūpamasukhasambidrūpamamaspṛṣṭaduḥkhaṁ* . . .
> — *Bhakti Rasāyana* 1

See, what a co-ordination, what a wonderful harmony indeed! In this co-ordination *nirūpamasukha-sambidrūpamamaspṛṣṭa-duḥkhaṁ tamihamakhilatuṣṭyai śāstradṛṣṭyā vyanajmi*. Through the word *vyanajmi* he has revealed the entire savour, and, when he went to Vṛndāvana after composing these scriptures, he was engrossed in the very same Lord Kṛṣṇa —

> *avyāsaistu vaśīkṛtena manasā yannirguṇaṁ niṣkriyaṁ*
> *jyotiḥ kiñcana yogino yadi paraṁ paśyanti paśyantu te* ।
> *asmākaṁ tu tadeva locanacamatkārāya bhūyācciraṁ*
> *kālindīpulinodare kimapi yannīlaṁ maho dhāvati* ॥

In that place also, what a delightful description has been given by Madusūdana Sarasvatī. What implies here is that whatever is the savour of devotion, whichever savour is like *Śrīmad Bhāgavata*, the same savour also flows in the form of Gaṅgā. When the current of the savour is flowing in Kāśī then we cannot make a difference between the two aforesaid savours. Gaṅgā is flowing in Kāśī containing within it all the Śāstras, philosophies and savours. The people of Kāśī have enjoyed this savour in religious discourses of *ācārya*s in past. The erudite scholars like Karapātrī Jī Mahārāja had bestowed the people of Kāśī with their discourses. My honourable father Brajabhūṣaṇa Lāl Jī Mahārāja had close association with the Dharma Saṁgha. A number of religious programmes were organized in his time in Jodhpur. Nirañjanadeva Jī, Śaṅkarācārya Jī and Karpātrī Jī Mahārāja used to visit regularly and attended these programmes. In my childhood when I was a student, I used to visit these honourable scholars. Karapātrī Jī used to ask me about what I was studying. He often asked me to speak, prove, or utter some words. It was in this way that I enjoyed his presence. I have listened to him when he spoke on the *Śrīmad Bhāgavata* especially Rasapañcādhyāyī. He used to get thrilled and emotional and even tears rolled from his eyes. Whenever he delivered on this subject, he did not remember about time. Being an ascetic and erudite scholar of Monism he was engrossed in savour of devotion. He had also presented the savour of *līlā*s (the acts of a deity) of Bhagavān Śrī Kṛṣṇa.

What I mean here is that whatever work Ācārya Śaṅkara had started was followed by the later *ācārya*s who eventually brought the work to its completion. Among these Śrī Vallabhācārya Caraṇa also made his contribution. He had developed the system of service (*sevā*) on the basis of Vedic proof derived from the system of Vedic worship. There is big difference between worship and service and both have different systems. Worship is symbolic and service is manifestation, *na pratīke na hi saḥ* — which has been mentioned by Vyās Jī in *Brahmasūtra* (4.1.4). He explains the difference between the worship and service systems. In the worship system we establish some symbol. In that symbol an invocation is made through Vedic *mantra*s and after the invitation god appears there. Then follows the worship and formal conclusion of worship. Thereafter, things become normal again. One can notice that during worship the worshipper takes a betelnut and then invites Gaṇeśajī. At first he worships Gaṇapati and then the worship is formally concluded. This worship system that concludes with *ādau gaṇapati pūjanam* has been mentioned as *tadeva brahma tvaṁ viddhi nedaṁ yadidamupāsate* in *Kenopaniṣad* (1.4-8).

In the worship system we attain *nirguṇa para-Brahma.* But in the service system the appearance of God-like is evident. In this system worship and its concluding rites have no place. It has only the presence of God in person as because the *līlā* of Bhagavān is in fact symbolic of God. Thus God is seen in person in this system and also His *līlā* as well. The *sūtra, lokavattu līlā kaivalyam* has been mentioned in the *Brahma-Sūtras* (2.1.33). *Bhagavatsvarūpa, bhagavallīlā, bhagvallīlāpadārtha,* everything has His appearance. So according to the doctrine of *viruddhadharmāśraya* you can see that all the Vedas have been revealed by all *ācāryas*. In the same way Śrī Vallabhācārya revealed the doctrine of *viruddhadharmāśraya* as the last link of this chain. According to this doctrine Bhagavān Śrī Kṛṣṇa is the Ultimate *Brahman,* the Supreme Being, and He has established the service system of Śrī Kṛṣṇa. His little appearance has Ultimate power — *śamo nāgena śamo maśakena, aṇoraṇīyān mahatomahīyān.* This little appearance also has the unlimited power —

> *tokena jīvaharaṇa yadalūkikāyāḥ traimāsikasya padā śakaṭo-*
> *pavṛttaḥ* ।
> *yadriṅgatā 'ntargatena divispṛśorvā unmūlanam tvitarathārjuna-*
> *yorna bhāvyam* ॥
> — *Bhāgavata* 2.7.27

Bhagavān Śuka said, *tokena jīvaharaṇam yat alaukikāyāḥ* and *traimāsikasya padā śakaṭo'pavṛttaḥ*. Body of a child of three months has a little foot and very soft, it doesn't has the power to overturn a cart. But the feet of Bhagavān have that power. Thus through the description of *viruddha-dharmāśraya*, on the basis of the *Śrīmad Bhāgavata* and accomplished by the gathering of the five *ācāryas*, enables the entire Indian philosophy to attain its completeness here. In the same way the literature of Braja became rich here. It has depth of feeling and is full of savour as well as philosophy. Sūradāsa who was one of the famous Aṣṭasakhās (the eight Bhakta poets) had composed those *padas* (couplets) which have significance, philosophy and depth of feelings. There is a *pada* that describes the flute playing of Bhagavān Śrī Kṛṣṇa —

> *aisī vaṅśī bajī nava ghana meṁ vyāpa rahī* ।
> *mahāmunina kī samādhi lāgī bhayo brahmanāda tahāṁ uṭhata āhlāda jahāṁ.*

The sound of Śrī Kṛṣṇa's flute resonates with *Brahman*. Such poetry is full of feeling and contains ultimate philosophy too. It cannot be detached from them. God becomes dependent on devotees, although He is supreme and unrestrained. He will act as the devotees desire, in spite of the fact that He is the Lord and we are His servants to carry out the orders of Lord. But when the savour exceeds, God begins to act as per wishes of devotees. He keeps the vow of the devotees and breaks His own.

> *svanigamamapahāya matpratijñāmamṛtamadhikartumavapluto rathasthaḥ* ।
> *dhṛtarathacaraṇo 'bhyāccaladgurhaririva hantumibhaṁ gatottarīyaḥ* ॥
> — *Bhāgavata* 1.9.37

God had said to Arjuna, *kaunteya pratijānīhi na me bhaktaḥ praṇaśyati* (*Gītā* 9.31). What a depth is seen in this sentence. God seems to be taking a vow here, but in fact God himself is not taking the vow — *kaunteya pratijānīhi*, it means, O! Arjuna you take a vow that my devotee will never be ruined, *na me bhaktaḥ praṇaśyati*. Here God is not taking the vow because had it been His vow then He would had to break it sometimes in favour of His disciple. But if it is the vow of the devotee then it would never break, it is then inviolable. Bhīṣma took the vow that he would compel Bhagavān to raise the arm. It was whose vow that succeeded? It was the vow of Bhīṣma, not of Bhagavān Śrī Kṛṣṇa that remained inviolable. As such Śrī Kṛṣṇa said, *kaunteya pratijānīhi*. O! Arjuna you take vow that my devotee will never be ruined. What it implies is that a deep co-ordination exist here; what a great difference between the soul and the Brahma, what a great difference between the shared and the sharer. God becomes dependent on soul, the shared.

. . . when there is an excess, such situation occurs and sometimes obverse too. God himself is in the form of *bhagavat-svarūpa*. For His devotees He even assumes the aspect of a girl and arrives as a girl-friend. There is a reference in the narration of Candrāvalī Jī that God, disguised as girl, arrives to deceive him. He even delighted him in that form. What does it mean? It is in fact only an act of gratifying or rewarding His devotee. It is also a pleasure of savour that God provided His devotee to experience.

These charming feelings are expressed in *Śrīmad Bhāgavata* and later on by the famous Aṣṭasakhās. Among these feelings I am reminded of an episode which has been described in a small poem of an unknown poet. This describes Bhagavān's appearance in the aspect of a girl-friend —

> *vithurī ghuṅgharālī laṭeṅ mukha pe alakāvali sājī avārani meṅ* ।
> *lakhi āṅkhana kī kajarāri chaṭā carcā baḍhi jāya lavārana meṅ* ॥
> *sakhi sāñca ko āñca nahīn sajanī yaha bāta kahūṅgī hajārana meṅ* ।
> *yadi nanda lalā tuma hote lalī to churī cala jāti bajārana meṅ* ॥

Climax of beauty, climax of love and climax of appearance, everything is entrusted in God. In whichever form He appears He bestows upon everyone bliss as per his entitlement.

I mean to say that in principle, the doctrines of all our *ācārya*s are similar. We may consider Tulasīdāsa to elucidate our point of view. The words — *sevaka sevibhāva binu bhavanatare ura māri* — were composed by Tulasīdāsa. These also explain the same point that God bestows delight and savour in the very same manner as a person praises Him. God bestows bliss upon a person according to his entitlement. He makes no demarcation among His devotees.

Kāśī has been called the cultural kingdom of India. All the currents of Indian culture join here. All the people from different parts of India enjoy the festivals, functions, etc., together.

It is Kāśī where all the streams join. All the *ācārya*s have expounded their philosophy from this city. Ācārya Vallabhā's birthplace is Champaran (ancient campāranya), near Raipur in Chhatisgarh, but his region of action is Kāśī. He was married in Kāśī, assumed *yajñopavīta* (sacred thread) here and even had his learning here. He participated in *śāstrārtha* (a doctrinal debate) in Kāśī, and *patrāvalambana śāstrārtha* was also performed at the doorstep of Viśvanātha Jī in Kāśī. He composed the *Subodhinī Ṭīkā* and also performed discourses on the *Śrīmad Bhāgavata* in the same Kāśī at the home of Seṭh Puruṣottamadāsa. The seat at Pancaganga Ghat in the present was the place where his marriage was performed. And at last there is a place called Āśrama-vyāmoha Līlā where according to our sect, Mahāprabhu Vallabhācārya took *jalasamādhi* (loss of life by drowning) in the Gaṅgā. His seat is still in existence at Hanuman Ghat in Kāśī. Thus, almost all the *ācārya*s expounded their doctrines here. Though endowed with all sorts of wealth, Kāśī even today cannot be recognized without Gaṅgā and the current of this holy river is flowing in Kāśī assimilating all the cultures and religions.

3

Splendour of Kāśī in Mahābhārata

Pranati Ghosal

vārāṇasyāḥ paraṁ sthānaṁ na bhūtaṁ na bhaviṣyati[1]

THERE is hardly any city in the world which can claim greater antiquity, greater continuity and greater popular veneration as Kāśī, so-to-say Varanasi, has enjoyed. It has been a holy city for at least three millenniums. No other city in India arouses so much religious emotion in the Hindus as Kāśī does. To each and every Hindu mind it represents great and unbroken traditions of religious sanctity and learning. It represents a miniature of Hindu life through the ages in all its great complexities and traditions.[2] In order to glorify this city Sister Nivedita has written:

> This is not only Canterbury for Hindus but at the same time Oxford to them. The sanctity of Kāśī is thousand times more than the Vatican city of Roman Catholics.
>
> — *Footfalls of Indian History*, II, p. 43

In our tradition we find almost all the Śāstras (including Vedas, Epics and Purāṇas) have eulogized and glorified Kāśī with high rapture and ecstacy.

Kāśī, as a seat of learning, is well-known since Brahmanic and Upanishadic period. Here not only brāhmaṇas but kṣatriyas also (who were normally martials and admini-

1. *Kūrma Purāṇa*, 1.29.63.
2. P.V. Kane, *History of Dharmaśāstra*, vol. IV, p. 618.

strators) were erudite scholars. The *BU*[3] has recorded the story of *dṛpta Bālāki*, who went to Kāśīrāja Ajātaśatru, with a desire to instruct him Supreme Knowledge, but ultimately himself was harassed by king's keen knowledge at every step of the same topic. At last he had to learn this lesson from the king. The same narration has been traced in the *Kauṣītaki Upaniṣad*[4] also with a slight variation.

The *Mahābhārata* has given us a lot of information about Kāśī, its history and geographical boundary, its kings in different ages, their relation to Kuru-Pāṇḍava scion and vice versa.

A detailed study of the passages of *Mbh*[5] has revealed two other names of Kāśī, i.e., Varanasi and Avimukta. In the Anuśāsana Parva of *Mbh* Bhīṣma the grandfather had instructed Yudhiṣṭhira on various topics. In course of his discussion, he had given a chronology of kings of Kāśī in different ages.[6] Thus we find names of Bhaimaseni Haryaśva → Sudeva → Divodāsa → Pratardana. Further, the names of Dīrghajihvā, Vṛṣadarbha, Uśīnara, Pururavas, Puru, Bhīmasena, Sarvasena, etc., have been recorded in the *Mbh*[7] as rulers of Kāśī in various ages. According to the narration of Bhīṣma, first we come across the name of Bhaimaseni Haryaśva, who adorned the throne of Kāśī and was assassinated by a Haihaya prince.[8] After him, his son Sudeva ascended the throne and in course of time had faced the same lot.[9] Next to him was Divodāsa (*Mbh* 13.30.15), the founder king of Varanasi. Having

3. *Bṛhadāraṇyaka Upaniṣad*, 2.1.1.
4. *Kauṣītaki Upaniṣad*, 4.1.
5. (i) *Kāśī* : *Mbh* 1.112.29; 2.30.6; 5.30.31; etc.
   (ii) *Vārāṇasī* : *Mbh* 3.84.78; 5.50.41; 13.30.16-18.
   (iii) *Avimukta* : *Mbh* 3.84.79.
6. *Ibid.*, 5.117.1; 5.117.6; 13.30.10-15; etc.
7. *Ibid.*, 1.67.40; 1.95.32; 5.117.1; 13.32.4-9; etc.
8. *Ibid.*, 13.30.10-12.
9. *Ibid.*, 13.30.13-14.

considered the ultimate fate of his ancestores and mighty prowess of Haihaya princes, he became determined to protect his motherland and consulted Indra. Under his instruction he rebuilt Varanasi. As a defensive measure he fortified the city, made it thickly populated, adorned it with shops, marts, all sorts of articles and other necessary provisions. In course of time it was so flourished and developed that it resembled Amarāvatī[10] (i.e., the capital city of Indra). As regards the geographical boundary of Varanasi, we find that this city extended from the northern bank of Ganges to the southern bank of Gomatī (*Mbh* 13.30.10). From the different names of the same place and description of well-furnished Varanasi city, it appears that Kāśī was the original name of the whole region. Later on Varanasi was established by Divodāsa as its capital city and a specific holy area (i.e., the central part of Varanasi) was called Avimukta. Most probably because of the great sanctity of this place, in some places the whole city has been identified with this name (Avimukta).

Now let us see Kāśīrāja's attitude towards Pāṇḍavas. Dr. Moti Chandra[11] in his work has remarked that Kāśīrāja was a close friend to Yudhiṣṭhira. Because of this intimacy, at the time of Abhimanyu's marriage he had accompanied the marriage party at Upaplavya city with a large number of soldiers.[12] His affection towards Pāṇḍavas is further proved by the fact that at the time of the great Kuru-Pāṇḍava war he had supported the Pāṇḍava side and joined them with thirty thousand soldiers.[13] According to the instruction of Yudhiṣṭhira, this group of army had fought against Kauravas under the leadership of Dhṛṣṭaketu, the king of Cedi.[14] Kāśīrāja

---

10. *Ibid.*, 13.30.15-18.
11. Moti chandra, *Kāśī kā Itihāsa*, p.25.
12. *kāśīrājaśca śaivyaśca prīyamāṇau yudhiṣṭhire* ।
    akṣauhiṇībhyāṁ sahitā vāgatau pṛthivī patau ॥ — *Mbh*, 4.72.16
13. *Mbh*, 5.50.41; 5.196.2; 6.25.5; etc.
14. *Ibid.*, 5.196.1-2.

himself was one of the great leaders because he was a competent warrior.[15] Their entire group was devastated by Bhīṣma.[16] Further, at the time of Yudhiṣṭhira's Horse-sacrifice when the sacrificial horse reached Kāśī, he didn't arrest it but allowed it to pass through his country.[17]

From the history of Kāśī, on the basis of references (as they have been recorded in different places of *Mbh*), we find that kings of different countries had so much attraction towards Kāśī that almost all of them (e.g., Kṛṣṇa, Bhīṣma, Pāṇḍu, Bhīma, Sahadeva, Karṇa, Bharata, etc.) had visited the place either to invade or to establish matrimonial relation or on their way to pilgrimage. In the Droṇa Parva,[18] Dhṛtarāṣṭra while narrating the feats of Śrī Kṛṣṇa referred to the Lord's victory over Kāśī and other countries. Again in the Udyoga Parva,[19] we find that once Kṛṣṇa made Varanasi a prey to fire. But we must remember that the above remark is not applicable about Lord Kṛṣṇa, because his motive of burning Varanasi was not to invade it but just to defend Dvārakā from the attack of a fiend. According to the narration of *Viṣṇu Purāṇa* (5.34) once Lord Vāsudeva was challenged by a Pauṇḍra King who was Vāsudeva by name only. He was so puffed up by the sycophant people that he believed to have assumed all the emblems of Śrī Kṛṣṇa and as such challenged him in a war almost arrogantly. Lord Kṛṣṇa accepted the challenge and next day He proceeded towards Pauṇḍra region. On receiving this message Kāśīrāja who was a friend to the false Vāsudeva, came to help him. But in the battlefield both Pauṇḍraka Vāsudeva and Kāśīrāja were killed by Śrī Kṛṣṇa. Here the story didn't end but took a new turn. After some time

15. *Ibid.*, 5.50.41; 6.50.57; 7.25.45; etc.
16. *Ibid.*, 6.106.18-20.
17. *Ibid.*, 14.83.4.
18. *Ibid.*, 7.11.15.
19. *Ibid.*, 5.48.76.

Kāśīrāja's son, when he came to know that Śrī Kṛṣṇa had killed his father, was determined to slaughter Him. He started penance for Śiva. When the Deity was pleased, as a boon, he wanted from Him a means of devastating both Śrī Kṛṣṇa and His Dvārikāpurī. Śiva created a female fiend, who right at that moment proceeded towards Dvārakā to burn it away. On seeing this Kṛṣṇa hurled his wheel at that fiend. Now, the fiend being afraid tried to escape but, wherever she went the wheel chased her. The fiend tried to conceal herself in Varanasi but the wheel chased her there also; and every place where the wheel touched the fiend caught fire. Thus Varanasi (which was obstructed for Divinities[20]) was burnt and damaged. The same narration has been traced in the *Padma Purāṇa* (3.33-36), *Harivaṁśa Purāṇa* (3.97-100) and *Bhāgavata Purāṇa* (10.2.65-66) with slight variation.

As a king of Hastināpura, Bhīṣma reached Kāśī, on the occasion of Kāśīrāja's three daughters' *svayaṁvara* and abducted them before the assemblage of kings.[21] As a result there was a war between Bhīṣma and the kings assembled there (esp. with Śālva who was determined to marry the eldest princess Ambā) but everybody was defeated by Bhīṣma. Besides, Bhīṣma, in the course of his invasion reached Kāśī and conquered the country.[22] Further, we have already mentioned that Yudhiṣṭhira's sacrificial horse passed through Kāśī.[23] Not only Yudhiṣṭhira but Bhīma also, before Yudhiṣṭhira's *Rājasūya* sacrifice, set out for invasion and conquered Kāśī and other countries.[24] Apart from this, in the Ādi Parva[25] Vaiśampāyana narrates that at the time of Arjuna's birth Kuntī received a divine prophecy that this new-born baby will conquer Kāśī

20. *Skanda Purāṇa,* Kāśī Khaṇḍa, ch. 43.
21. *Ibid.,* 1.102.3-53.
22. *Ibid.,* 1.112.29.
23. *Ibid.,* 14.83.4.
24. *Ibid.,* 2.30.6; 5.50.19.
25. *Ibid.,* 1.122.40.

and Arjuna did so in later years. Sahadeva also, when he set out for invasion, won over Kāśī.[26] In this connection we may refer to Karṇa's invasion of Kāśī; he overpowered Kāśīrāja for the sake of Duryodhana.[27]

But a point must be remembered here that the attitude of the kings (who reached Kāśī) was not always hostile. Sometimes they came here to establish matrimonial relations also. As already mentioned Bhīṣma reached Kāśī with a desire to collect bride for his younger brother. It is true that he had carried away the princesses by force before the kings, but when he came to know that Ambā was already engaged with Śālva, he had allowed her to depart and got the two other princesses married to his younger brother Vicitravīrya.[28] Besides Bhīṣma, Bhīmasena in later ages married Balandharā, the princess of Kāśī.[29] Further, Bharata's (son of Duṣyanta) marriage with Kāśīrāja Sarvasena's daughter Sunandā may be mentioned here as another similar instance.[30]

From the very early period, Varanasi has been sanctified by its resident-hermits, saints and learned persons like Tūlādhāra, Saṁvartta, Asita Devala, Jaigiṣavya, etc. Among them Tūlādhāra has been mentioned as an embodiment of *dharma*. It is interesting to note here that in spite of being a petty trader Tūlādhāra[31] knew the true essence of *dharma*, and his glory and wisdom was known even to the *gandharva*s and *piśāca*s in the atmospheric region.[32] Another remarkable figure

---

26. *Ibid.*, 5.50.37.
27. *Ibid.*, 8.8.19.
28. (i) *tāḥ sarvaguṇa sampannā bhrātā bhrātre yavīyase* ।
    bhīṣmo vicitravīryāya pradadau vikramā hṛthaḥ ॥ — *Mbh*, 1.102.58

    (ii) *ambikāmbālike bhārye prādād bhratre yavīyase* ।
    bhīṣmo vicitravīryāya vidhidṛṣṭena karmaṇā ॥ — *Mbh*, 1.102.65
29. *Ibid.*, 1.95.77.
30. *Ibid.*, 1.95.32.
31. *Ibid.*, 12.261.8; 12.261.43; 12.262.2-6.
32. *Ibid.*, 12.261.7; 12.261.42.

was Saṁvartta, the young brother of Devaguru Bṛhaspati.[33] The Āśvamedhika Parva (6.18-7.22) in the narrative of king Marutta states that Saṁvartta roamed everywhere in Varanasi like a half-minded man. Everyday he visited Avimukta *kṣetra* with a desire to worship Lord Śiva (*Mbh* 14.6.22). Though a fanatic in appearance he knew all details about sacrifice (*yajñatattva*). Under the instruction of Nārada, king Marutta came to Kāśī, identified Saṁvartta and consecrated him as his priest. Further the Anuśāsana Parva[34] informs us about hermit Jaigīṣavya, who practised here rigorous penance for Śiva. The Lord being pleased with the sage bestowed eight Supernatural Powers (*aṣṭasiddhi*).

Since hoary past, Varanasi has been marked as a holy centre of pilgrimage. In order to glorify its splendour the Vana Parva[35] in the context of *tīrthayātrā* narrates that Varanasi is such a sanctified place, where with the aid of holy bath in the *kapilāhrada* and worship of Lord Śiva, the pilgrim can attain the results of performing the *Rājasūya* sacrifice. The central part of Kāśī was called Avimukta; it was so highly sanctified that only a visit to this place could release a person even from the serious offence like Brāhmaṇicide.[36] Death at this place was very desirable for religious-minded people; because people at that time believed that if a person expires here he would directly attain Final Beatitude.[37]

Thus, we find a lot of information about Kāśī, scattered all over the *Mbh* (especially in Ādi, Vana, Udyoga, Śānti and Anuśāsana Parva). It appears that after the scanty references

33. *Ibid.*, 14.7.9-11.

34. *Ibid.*, 13.18.37.

35. *tato vārāṇasīṁ gatvā arcayitvā vṛṣadhvajam* ।
kapilāhrade naraḥsnātvā rājasūyam avāpnuyāt ॥ — *Mbh*, 3.84.78

36. *avimuktaṁ samāsādya tīrthasevī kurūdvahaḥ* ।
darśanād devadevasya mucyate brahmahatyayā ॥ — *Mbh*, 3.84.80

37. *prāṇān utsṛjya tatvaiva mokṣaṁ prāpnoti mānavaḥ* ॥ — *MBH* 3.84.80

found in the Upaniṣads, probably the *Mbh* provides the earliest detailed account of Kāśī, even before Purāṇas. Among all the old cities of India Kāśī is the holiest and one of the most important centres of learning and culture. The city has been enjoying a unique celebrity right from the Vedic time. The *Mbh* upholds this tradition and gives a detailed account of its glory from various viewpoints. Recognition of Kāśī as the cultural capital of India can be traced back to the *Mbh* wherein its material and spiritual importance both find a grand exposition. Common people like Tulādhāra the trader, Saṁvartta, the crazy seeker of Truth, along with competent rulers like Divodāsa, Uśīnara, etc., have determined the unique character of this old city. Attraction of Avimukta for the seekers of Final Beatitude also plays an important role in the splendour of Kāśī — which may be called a beautiful confluence of Religion and Knowledge. This splendour has attracted all people towards Kāśī through the ages up to this day. P.V. Kane,[38] while paying his tribute towards Kāśī, has written:

> Celebrity of Kāśī is far greater than that Rome had for Christians or Jerusalem for Jews or Mecca for the Mohammedans.

The same truth is reflecetd in the observation of another modern scholar:

> Banāras is a magnificent city, rising form the western bank of the River Ganges, where the River takes a crescent sweep towards the north. There is little in the world to compare with the splendor of Banāras, seen from the river at dawn. The rays of early-morning sun, spread across the river and strike the high-banked face of this city which Hindus call Kāshī — the Luminous, the City of Light.[39]

---

38. P.V. Kane, *History of Dharmaśāstra,* vol. III, p. 645.
39. Diana L. Eck, Banāras — City of Light, p. 3.

Bibliography

(*Śrīmad*) *Bhāgavata Purāṇa,* ed. with Śridharī Ṭīkā, Varanasi: Chaukhamba Surabharati Prakashan, 1988.

———, trans. C.L. Goswami, 2 vols. Gorakhpur: Gita Press, 1997.

Chandra, Moti, *Kāśī kā Itihāsa,* Varanasi : Vishvavidyalaya Prakashan, 1985.

Diana L. Eck, *Banaras — City of Light,* London : Routledge & Kegan Paul, 1983.

P.V. Kane, *History of Dharmaśāstra,* Gov. Oriental Series, Class B, no. 6, vol. III, 3rd edn., 1993; vol. IV, 2nd edn., 1991. Poona : Bhandarkar Oriental Research Institute.

Mahābhārata, ed. & tr. Pt. Ram Narayan Dutt Shastri Pandeya, 6 vols. Gorakhpur : Gita Press, 1955-94.

Mahābhārata kī Nāmānukramaṇikā, ed. V.S. Agrawal, Gorakhpur : Gita Press, 1958.

Vettam Mani, *Puranic Encyclopaedia,* Delhi : MLBD, 1996.

(*Śrī*) *Padma Mahāpurāṇam,* ed. Pt. Nag Sharan Simha, 4 vols., Delhi: Nag Publishers, 1984.

(*Śrī*) *Skanda Mahāpurāṇam,* ed. Pt. Nag Sharan Simha, 7 vols., Delhi: Nag Publishers, 1986-87.

Acharya Pt. Baladeva Upadhyaya, *Kāshī kī Pāṇḍitya Paramparā* (1200 AD.-1950 AD). Varanasi : Vishvavidyalaya Prakashan, 1983.

(*Śrī*) *Viṣṇu Mahāpurāṇam,* ed. Pt. Nag Sharan Simha, Delhi : Nag Publishers, 1985.

4

The Mediaeval Vaiṣṇava Bhakti Movement and Kāśī

Vasudeva Singh

Significance of Vaiṣṇava Movement

THE mediaeval Vaiṣṇava Bhakti movement was a unique incident in the history of India. That movement not only continued for about three centuries but has also influenced the religious persuasions of India to date. This movement has been significant not only in the field of religion; has also given new directions from the viewpoint of cultural and social aspects.

The Vaiṣṇava Bhakti movement of the fourteenth-fifteenth centuries was not limited to one or two regions but it seems to pervade the entire country. Being astonished by the profundity and extensiveness of this movement, Grierson wrote,

> We find ourselves in front of such a religious movement which is the most extensive among all the movements in India. Even it is more extensive than the movement of Bauddha *dharma,* because it is influential even these days. In that era *dharma* became the matter of emotion in spite of knowledge. From here we came to know the fields of mysticism and rapture and have interaction with such souls which do not belong to the tradition of the erudite *paṇḍita*s of Kāśī, but are comparable to the mediaeval European saints like Barnard, Thomas A. Campeen, and Saint Theresa.

In fact, this movement had influenced all walks of life of Indians, worldly or spiritual. It has great significance from all the viewpoints such as religion, philosophy and culture. The poet followers of *nirguṇa* and *saguṇa* doctrines have influenced the life values deeply. The poets, who were followers of the *nirguṇa* doctrine, had diffused the message of humanism opposing all kinds of narrowness, external conducts and deceitful behaviour and established all creatures on a common platform. On the other hand, the poets following the *saguṇa* doctrine diffused a new message in perspective of the ancient Indian traditions. Nurture of dignity and a great devotee of Rāma, the poet Tulasīdāsa had presented such a social example whose influence is present even today. He showed the ideal path of life to Indians in the times of social and cultural disorders and anarchy and gave a new insight to the people suffering from separated family relations and turbulence for trifling selfishness. *Rāmacaritamānasa* mentioned what sort of an ideal family system should be, what sort of relations should be between the father and the son, brothers, husband and wife, servant and master, and teacher and taught, and how the different classes of society like the rich, the poor, the householders and ascetics could follow an ideal life?

Śaiva Sect

The Śaiva *dharma* was in high repute before this movement. Śiva was the main deity up to the seventh-eighth centuries in this country. Most of the royal families were followers of the Śaiva *dharma.* He was worshipped almost in the whole of the country in the forms of several sects, just as Pāśupata, Kaula, Kāpālika, Lakulīśa, Vīra Śaiva, etc.

The Mihira family, Harṣa, Candela family, Devavarmā, Madan Varmā, kings of Cauhāna and Gahaḍavāla families were followers of Śiva and Śaivas had extensive influence in the south also. Śiva temples existed from Kāśī in the north to far south. Huen-T-sang, a pilgrim from China, visited India in the early seventh century and narrated the religious and cultural situation in India in those days. He has mentioned that worship of Śiva in Pāśupata sect was in vogue and there were hundreds of temples of Paśupati in Makarān. Maheśvara was worshipped in Jalandhar, Ahicchatra (Ram Nagar), Kapittha, Kannauj and also from the river Indus to the river Sutlej in Punjab and temples were erected. There were about 100 Śiva temples and more than 10,000 devotees in Varanasi.[1] After Ayodhyā, Goddess Durgā was worshipped in adjacent areas of Gaṅgā where human sacrifice was performed annually. The Kāpālikas had extensive influence in the eastern regions and they wore necklaces of bones. There were many Paśupati temples in Mālwā in the west. Worship of Śiva was popular in southern India. Pt. Baldeva Upadhyaya records:

> The region namely Tamil was the dominating centre of Śaiva sect. There were four prominent *ācārya*s among the 84 Śaiva saints. Their names are — Apayār, Jñāna Sambandha, Sundera Mūrti and Maṇika Vācaka. They were founders of the four important doctrines of Śaiva *dharma* in Tamil region namely — *caryā, kriyā, yoga* and *jñāna*. Their emergence time was the seventh or eighth centuries. Earlier, Nakkīra (Prathama Śataka), Kaṇṇaya (Dvitīya Śataka) and Tirūmūlara had propagated the Śaiva sect.[2]

Vaiṣṇava Bhakti Movement

But coming to the eighth century Śaiva influence gradually decreased and Vaiṣṇava Bhakti movement gained in strength. Several *ācārya*s founded different sects in south India. Earlier there was predominance of Āḷvār *bhakta*s whose is assigned from fourth to nineth centuries. Āḷvārs were saints of high repute and were mainly engrossed in adoration of God. They have been assumed to be 12 in number, including a woman

---

1. Tarachand, *Influence of Islam on Indian Culture*, p. 7.
2. *Bhāratīya Darśana*, pp. 572-73.

named Aṇḍāla. She was famous as "Mīrā" of south. The word āḷvār means — absorbed. Those saints are called Āḷvārs who were immersed in the sea of spiritual knowledge. Śrīnātha Muni collected their *padas* under the title *Divya Prabandham* at the end of the ninth century. Generally, they are considered *saguṇa bhaktas*, but they were worshippers of *nirguṇa Brahman* too. According to their sect there is no conflict between *saguṇa* and *nirguṇa*.

After Āḷvār *bhaktas*, several *ācāryas* combined adoration with the philosophical form in the south. Śaṅkarācārya was a unique and erudite scholar in his time. He conquered all the anti-Vedic forces by virtue of his remarkable skill in speech and supernatural brilliance and revived the spiritual and Upaniṣadic tradition leading to knowledge. A new spiritual power upsurged with his influence, but his intricate monistic theories could not attract the people from the viewpoint of worship. The support which is needed by an emotional *bhakta* is totally absent from Śaṅkara's doctrine. For the same reason later *ācāryas* refuted his Monism and proved *bhakti* to be better than knowledge. Among those *ācāryas*, Nimbārkācārya, Madhvācārya, Rāmānujācārya, Viṣṇusvāmī and Vallabhācārya were prominent. Generally, all of them were Vaiṣṇavas (devotees of Viṣṇu). Several sects like Śrī, Sanak, Rudra, came into existence with their efforts. Later on those sects were also divided into many branches. Rāmānandī sect, Vallabha sect, doctrines like Haridāsī, Harivyāsī, Caitanya, etc., emerged from the very same sects. Bhakti literature of Hindi is a product of the influence of the very same *ācāryas* of the south. Accepting this fact, Kabīra said —

bhaktī drāviḍa ūpajī lāe rāmānanda ।
paragaṭa kiyā kabīra ne sāta dīpa navakhaṇḍa ॥

Apart from it several other sects also arose like the Mahāpuruṣiyā *dharma* in Assam, Sahajīyā in Bengal, Pañcasakhā in Orissa, Mahānubhāvī Bārakarī in Maharashtra. Rajasthan was resounded with the songs of love of the *bhaktas* like Mīrā, who were worshippers of love. Thus, we see that in the mediaeval times the entire country was immersed in the savour of adoration (*bhakti*).

Contribution of Kāśī

Kāśī is an ancient city of the world. It is called "Sanātana Kāśī" (eternal Kāśī). The word Kāśī means which illuminates the knowledge, *kāśyate prakāśyate jñānaṁ anena iti kāśī*. Many of the *ṛṣis*, *munis* and *ācāryas* had visited Kāśī to illuminate and prove their knowledge. For the same reason Kāśī has the pride of being the oldest city of knowledge, religion and culture. *Harivaṁśa Purāṇa* mentions that it was dwelled by the king Kāśī, the descendant of Bharat. So it was named Kāśī. Gosvāmī Tulasīdāsa called it *"Mukti Kṣetra"* (region of salvation) and *"Jñāna Kṣetra"* (region of knowledge) —

> *mukti janma mahi jāni, jñāna khāni atha hāni kara* ।
> *jahaṁ basa saṁbhu bhavāni, so kāsī seia kasa na* ॥

Kāśī has been named as Varanasi, Avimukta, Ānanda Kānana and Śmaśāna or Mahāśmaśāna too. In ancient times Kāśī was *janapada* and Varanasi as its capital. Later, both the words became synonymous. The city, situated between the rivers Varuṇā and Asī, is called Varanasi.

The discovery of the evidence of the significance of Kāśī started from the Vedic era. Kāśī has been mentioned in Saṁhitās, Brāhmaṇic scriptures and Upaniṣads. Most of the Upaniṣads were composed in Kāśī. Apart from Sanskrit literature, the grandeur of Kāśī has been found mentioned in Sanskrit folk too. Beside Sanskrit literature, the grandeur of Kāśī has been mentioned in the Bauddha and Jaina scriptures too. Gautama Buddha had promoted *dharmacakra* (wheel of *dharma*) at Sārnāth, near Kāśī. Jaina *Tīrthaṅkara* Parśvanātha was born in Kāśī and his temple stands at his birthplace near the Vijayanagara Mahal, Bhelupur. The 11th Jaina *Tīrthaṅkara* Śreyāṁśanātha was also born at Sārnāth near Kāśī.

The city has been the centre of religion (*dharma*), learning, and spiritualism since ancient times; and a prominent centre of knowledge of different sorts, religion (*dharma*) and philosophy, culture and literature in mediaeval period too, and renowned saints from far off areas thronged and guided the Indians with their *sārasvata-sādhanā* (accomplishment of knowledge). Śaṅkarācārya, born at a remote place in Kerala, arrived in Kāśī during the ninth century. He had authored his commentary on the *Brahma-Sūtras* here. After Śaṅkarācārya, evidence of the arrival of several other scholars from south, like Yāmunācārya, Rāmānujācārya, Nimbārkācārya, Madhvācārya, have been found. Mahāprabhu Vallabhācārya had his initiation and learning in the very same Kāśī. In the same way Mahāprabhu Caitanya, the founder of Gauḍīya sect; the famous saints of Maharastra like Ekanātha, Jñāneśvara, Tukārāma, Svāmī Rāmadāsa; and founder of Sikha *dharma*, Guru Nānakdevajī, also visited Kāśī.

Role of Kāśī in Vaiṣṇava Bhakti Movement

Kāśī has played a prominent role in the diffusion of Vaiṣṇava *bhakti* movement. Kāśī and Vṛndāvana were two prominent centres for *bhakti* in mediaeval times. Kāśī was centre of Rāma *bhakti* and Vṛndāvana of Kṛṣṇa *bhakti*. Svāmī Rāmānanda founded *nirguṇa-saguṇa* forms of Śrī Rāma in Kāśī. His 22 disciples, like Kabīra, Raidāsa, worshipped formless (*nirākāra*) Śrī Rāma whereas Gosvāmī Tulasīdāsa was devoted to the *saguṇa* form of Rāma, a son of king Daśaratha. It is to be noted that the disciples (*bhaktas*) of Kṛṣṇa made His birthplace their sphere of functions, whereas the disciples of Rāma chose Kāśī as the centre for Rāma *bhakti* instead of Ayodhyā. Why? In fact, its main reason is the effort which was made by the saints to unite Śaivas and Vaiṣṇavas. The gradual decay of the Śaiva *dharma* and the progress of Vaiṣṇava *dharma* initiated conflicts between the Śaiva and the Vaiṣṇavas. In the mediaeval times the conflict between the followers of the two sects increased.

So the saints and ascetics expounded the unity between Rāma and Śiva to avoid the friction between the followers of the two sects. So they introduced praises of Śiva by Rāma and praises of Rāma by Śiva, and made Śiva's city, Kāśī, a prominent centre for Rāma *bhakti*. *Śrīrāmottaratāpanīyopaniṣad* mentioned that Śiva Himself recited *Rāma-Mantra* for thousands of *manvantaras* for bestowing salvation to the creatures. As a result Śrī Rāma fulfilled his wish —

śrī rāmasya manuṁ kāśyāṁ jajāpa vr̥ṣabhadhvajaḥ ।
manvantara sahasraistu japahomārcanādibhiḥ ॥
mumurṣordakṣiṇe karṇe yasya kasyāpi vā svayam ।
upadekṣyasi manmantraṁ sa mukto bhavitā śiva ॥
— *Śrī Rāmottaratāpanīyopaniṣad*, II.1, II.8

Nandī Purāṇa mentioned that no one knows as Bhagavān Śaṅkara knew, the nature, influence and significance of Bhagavān Śrī Rāma.

jānāti rāmanāmastu paratvaṁ girijāpatiḥ ।
tadanyo na vijānāti satyaṁ satyaṁ vaco mama ॥

Describing this fact Gosvāmī Tulasīdāsa also mentioned —

mahāmantra joi japat mahesū । *kāsī mukuti hetu upadesū* ॥

....

nāma prabhāvajāna siva nīko, kālakūṭa phalu dīnha amī ko.

The *Adhyātms Rāmāyaṇa* has been attributed to Śiva and he also proclaims that the name of Rāma has the capacity for bestowing salvation —

ahaṁ bhavannāmaguṇaiḥ kr̥tārtho vasāmi kāśyāmaniśaṁ bhavānyā ।
mumurṣamāṇasya vimuktaye'haṁ diśāmi mantraṁ tava rāma nāma ॥

Thus, it is clear that Śiva himself recited the *Rāma Tāraka Mantra* for thousands of years in Kāśī and acquired ability for bestowing salvation to the sensuous creatures. So which place could be a better centre for Rāma Bhakti than Kāśī?

Svāmī Rāmānanda

Following the same tradition Svāmī Rāmānanda (who himself is being assumed as *avatāra* of Rāma) accepted Kāśī as the centre for Rāma Bhakti. Svāmī Rāmānanda was one of the disciples in the tradition of Rāmānujācārya, the founder of "Śrī Vaiṣṇava sect," but he had changed several rites of this sect. Proclaiming the harmony and brotherhood in the social and religious fields, he brought into vogue the worship of Trimūrti, trinity of Rāma, Lakṣmaṇa and Sītā, in place of the worship of the image of Bhagvān Viṣṇu reclining on the snake, Śeṣa. He also exhorted *Śrī Rāma Tāraka mantra* (*rāṁ rāmāya namaḥ*). It has been said that at first Hanumān was initiated by the Jagatjananī (mother of the world) Sītā with the same *mantra*. So this sect was named as "Śrī Sampradāya or Rāmāvata Saṃpradāya." The ascetics, initiated into this sect, made several temples of Sītārāma in different parts of the country, among which "Śrī Nātha," embellished at Panchaganga Ghat in Kāśī is the original place of Rāmānandīya Śrī Vaiṣṇava Samāja.

Svāmī Rāmānanda accepted both the forms of Rāma, *saguṇa* and *nirguṇa*. He can be worshipped in any of the forms. Kabīra followed the *nirguṇa* form of Rāma while Tulasīdāsa the *saguṇa* form. Svāmī Rāmānanda also learned *yoga* from Rāghavānanda. *Siddhānta Pañcamātraṁ*, composed by Śrī Rāmānanda shows that *yoga* and love were united in his way of adoration.[3] It implies that the *sādhanā* system of *haṭha-yoga* was in practice on one hand and on the other hand imprint (*chāpa*), garland (*mālā*), mark (*tilaka*), accepted by the Vaiṣṇava *bhakta*s, were also in vogue. Śrī Rāmānanda spread the Rāma Bhakti combined with *yoga*. Anantānanda, the disciple of Rāmānanda also accepted the *bhakti* combined with *yoga*. But this adoration

3. Barthwal, *Yoga Pravāha*, pp. 2-3.

system was spread by his disciple Śrī Kr̥ṣṇa Dās Payahārī. There is a co-ordination between *bhakti* and *yoga* in the adoration system of Kabīradāsa too. The *bhakti* combined with *yoga*, which was obtained from Rāmānanda, detached Kabīradāsa from his predecessor Siddha and Nātha ascetics.

Svāmī Rāmānanda's significant contribution was the acceptance of Hindi, which was the language of the common people. Although Svāmī Rāmānanda composed the *Vaiṣṇava Matābja Bhāskara* and the *Śrī Rāmārcana Paddhati* in Sanskrit, most of his compositions are in Hindi. Title names of those compositions are — *Rāmarakṣā Stotra, Siddhānta Paṭala, Jñāna Līlā, Jñāna Tilaka* and *Yoga Cintāmaṇi*. Dr. Pitambara Barthwal edited those compositions under the title *Rāmānanda Kī Hindī Racanāyen*. He had composed a poem in praise of Hanumān and in Rajjabadāsa's collection, *Sarvāṅgī*, his following *pada* has been found:

> *hari binu janma vr̥thā khoyo re* ।
> *kahā bhayo ati māna baṛhāī, dhana, mada andha mati soyo re* ॥
> *ati utaṅga taru dekhi suhāyo, sevala kusuma suvā seyo re* ।
> *soī phala putra-kalatra viṣai-sukha anti sīsa ghuni-ghuni royo re* ॥
> *sumirana bhajana sātha kī saṅgati antari mana maila na dhoyo re* ।
> *rāmānanda ratana jama trāsa, śrīpati pada kāhe na joyo re* ॥

His significance is realized even today in the cultural and religious fields. In fact, Svāmī Rāmānanda would be remembered forever as a unique missionary of the adoration of Rāma, as a founder of harmony, friendship and humanism; as a reformer of national language, Hindi; and an uplifter of nationalism.

Kabīradāsa

It is believed that Svāmī Rāmānanda had 22 disciples. Among them the personality of Kabīra was most pervasive and splendid. He diffused the adoration of *nirguṇa* (beyond quality) and *nirākāra* (formless) Rāma on the strength of his deep accomplishment and meditation. He was initiated by Svāmī Rāmānanda. Although Kabīra was a worshipper of the *nirguṇa* form of Rāma, the meaning of *nirguṇa* was not similar to that of the Vedānta for him. *Nirguṇa Brahman*, mentioned in Vedānta cannot be worshipped. He never comes into contact. He is the base of the universe, yet does not create Itself. *Māyā* is the strength of the very same *nirguṇa*. He creates the cosmos and gets converted into *saguṇa*. Kabīra assumed the *Brahman* worthy of adoration. He can be called *saguṇa nirākāra* (virtuous and formless). Although beyond radiance, passion and indolence (*sat, rajas* and *tamas*), He combines several virtues. He is wise, kind, powerful and an ocean of joys. There are many merits in Rāma of Kabīra. Even if the seven seas would have converted into ink, all the forests into pen and the whole earth into paper, then also the complete description of the virtues of God is not possible —

> *sāta samunda kī masi karaun, lekhani saba banarāi* ।
> *dharatī saba kāgada karaun (tau) hari guna likhā na jāi* ॥
>
> — *Samudhāī ko aṅga*

In fact, Rāma for Kabīra is not present in the sense of form but in the sense of virtue. Form or shape is destructive, but Rāma is eternal, who neither takes birth nor does He die. As truth is unlimited, in the same way Rāma is unlimited too. In fact, Kabīra has been linked continuously with the Indian tradition of worship. The way in which he has described the adoration and narrations of the mythological great men, like Sanaka, Sanandana, Śiva, Brahmā, Nārada, Dhruva, Prahlāda, Vibhīṣaṇa, Śeṣanāga, Vaśiṣṭha, Vedavyāsa, Hanumān, Śukadeva, Sudāmā, devotees (*yogīs*) like Gorakhanātha, Bhartṛhari, Gopīcanda, etc., and also the preceding saints like Jayadeva, Nāmadeva, clearly indicates that he was not only deeply acquainted with the Indian religious tradition and culture as well as religious literature (*bhakti-sāhitya*), but was also influenced and linked with them in his spirit. Nārada, Vedavyāsa and Śukadeva have been famous devotees (*bhaktas*) in the field of adoration. Kabīra has presented them repeatedly as a proof for ratification of the significance of his adoration:

> *nārada vacana miṭhāsa kahata hai suka kaun puchaha jāī* ।
> *kahai kabīra rāme rami chūtahu nāhi ta būṛe bhāī* ॥
>
> — *pada,* 164-10.11

Thus, it is clear from the aforesaid description that Kabīra's adoration was of Vaiṣṇava. He was deeply influenced by the Vaiṣṇava tradition. According to Dr. Munshi Ram Sharma.

> A fact that is understood easily by the people through narrations and negotiations, could not be possible with mysterious fixations of philosophy. For this reason Kabīra accepted the *Hari Nāmāvalī* (names of God), *Bhakti Kathā*s (narrations belonging to adoration) and *Avatāra Līlā*s (acts of *avatāra*s) presented by mythological personalities unaltered. It seems that his aim was to inspire people towards God.[4]

Although he had not accepted the traditional Vaiṣṇava *bhakti* in its entirety, and has considered *nirguṇa* and formless to be worthy of adoration instead of *avātārī* Rāma and opposed Vaiṣṇava's *japa,* (garland) *mālā,* (imprint) *chāpa, tilaka* (sectarian mark), yet the *nāradī bhakti, navadhā bhakti, prapattimūlaka bhakti, bhāgavata bhakti, guru mahimā, nāma mahimā,* etc., are sufficiently present in his doctrine. He was a Vaiṣṇava *bhakta* in this respect.

Other Saints of Nirguṇa doctrine of Kāśī

Svāmī Rāmānanda's second important disciple Raidāsa or Ravidāsa was also born in a village near Maduvadiha in the west of Kāśī. He had gained enough fame in the society for his meditation and adoration of God. There are several kinds of supernatural and astonishing hearsay in vogue about him. It is said that impressed by his meditation, Jhālī, the Queen of Cittaur, took initiation from him in Kāśī.

---

4. *Bhakti Kā Vikās,* p. 432.

Raidāsa's 30 *padas* have been collected in the *Guru Grantha Sāhib* and a collection of his compositions has been published by the Velavediyar Press, Allahabad. His compositions reflect that he was a worshipper like Kabīra. His one *pada* is given below —

aba kaise chūṭe rāma nāma raṭa lāgī ।
prabhujī tuma candana hama pānī, jākī aṅga aṅga vāsa samānī ॥
prabhujī tuma ghana vana hama morā, jaise citavata canda cakorā ।
prabhujī tuma dīpaka hama bātī, jākī jyoti barai din rātī ॥
prābhujī tuma motī hama dhāgā, jaise sone milā sohāgā ।
prabhujī tuma svāmī hama dāsā, aisī bhakti karai raidasā ॥

Among other saints who followed the *nirguṇa* tradition and the evidence of whose arrival to Kāśī has been traced, Dādū and Sundaradāsa (Choṭe) were prominent. The place of spiritual accomplishment of Dādū has been believed to be Jaipur, but he stayed at Kāśī for some period. It is said that he was the sixth disciple of Rāmānanda.

Saint Sundaradāsa (Choṭe) was a disciple of Dādū Dayāla. His parents handed him to Dādū when he was six years old, but he could not live with his *guru* for a long because after some time Dādū expired. Thereafter, the responsibility of his bringing up and to get him initated came upon the two prominent disciples of Dādū, namely, Jagajīvana jī and Rajjabajī. They took him to Kāśī for learning. Here he learned literature and philosophy for 19 years (Saṁvat 1663 to 1682). He lived at Assi Ghat in Kāśī. Tulasīdāsa also lived there in those days. Saint Sundaradāsa obtained a lot of advantage from the presence of Gosvāmī Tulasīdāsa. By chance at the very same time the famous Saint and Jaina poet Banārasīdāsa also lived in Kāśī. Banārasīdāsa and Sundaradāsa used to discuss on religious and spiritual matters.

Tulasīdāsa

Kāśī has also been the centre of *saguṇa bhakti* of Śrī Rāma of which the most famous and brilliant poet was Gosvāmī Tulasīdāsa. No matter wherever he was born, his place of work was the very same Kāśī. The Middle Age was not only the period of disorder from the viewpoint of politics, but that was also a period of anarchy from the viewpoint of religion and culture. The dispute between *nirguṇa* and *saguṇa* was on climax in those days, and the followers of different sects like Śaiva, Śākta, Smārtta were also quarrelling with each other. Gosvāmī Tulasīdāsa tried to establish harmony between these sects. Main conflict was between Śaivas and Vaiṣṇavas. So he got the narration of *Rāmacaritamānasa* through the mouth of Śiva. He evolved a close relation between Rāma and Śiva. He proclaimed Śiva as attendant (*sevaka*), master (*svāmī*), and a friend (*sakhā*) of the husband of Sītā, *sevaka svāmī sakhā siya piya ke*. Tulasīdāsa's Rāma praised and worshipped Śiva and Śiva has been revealed praising Rāma. Besides, he even propagated the worship of Hanumān. He established 12 temples of Hanumān in Kāśī and promoted *Rāmalīlā* on the basis of his famous work *Rāmcaritamānasa* with the help of his friend Meghā Bhagata. We can see the scenes of *Rāmalīlā* in the month of Āśvina in several sectors of Kāśī even today. Among those, *Rāmalīlā* of Rāmanagar is the most famous.

5

Vaiṣṇava Image of Kāśī

Yugeshvara

BASICALLY Kāśī is the city of Śiva. It is difficult to say when and how the Vaiṣṇava sect originated here? Perhaps it is not necessary here but may be for those who believe in the rivalry between Śiva and Viṣṇu, the reason of which is not a conflict between Viṣṇu and Śiva, rather the casual conflict among their devotees from time to time. In fact, it is one and the secondless *Brahman*, who assumed the image of three forms (*tridhā*). Through this has been often established the harmony between Śiva and Viṣṇu instead of any conflict or tension. The Western scholars and the people under their influence feel pleasure on seeing such a conflict. There are one or two examples of this feeling, but even these are only illusions of conflict between Śiva and Viṣṇu as they represent God Who has no selfish motif. If there is no self interest, there cannot be a conflict. However, even if there is any conflict, among them, that is only for safeguarding the devotees. The ignorant worshippers sometimes quarrel with each other. Even God comes to help them. The gods pretend to struggle and such pretension is held as a conflict. Kāśī has been called by the name of Varanasi too. This city of Varanasi was once set on fire by Bhagavān Kṛṣṇa. This narration has been composed many times but its cause was not the conflict between Śiva and Kṛṣṇa. Actually Śiva bestows blessings without delay. As such, He often blessed the undeserving persons and monsters too. Hence, people think that Śiva is the god of monsters which is not true. He becomes pleased even with the little adoration of monsters and it is His *līlā*. They divide the duties. One deity blesses, the other destroys. Śiva protects Bāṇāsura, Rāvaṇa, etc., whereas Kṛṣṇa and Rāma kill them.

The cause for setting Varanasi on fire is totally different. Pauṇḍraka, King of Karuṣa, stayed with the king of Kāśī in those days. He was a bitter enemy of Kṛṣṇa. Śrī Kṛṣṇa killed Pauṇḍraka as well as the king of Kāśī. The son of King of Kāśī worshipped Śiva. Śiva was pleased with him and deployed his attendants in war. Kṛṣṇa's *cakra* set Varanasi on fire, but it did not create enmity between Kṛṣṇa and Śiva. There are several narrations similar to this episode. In those narrations Arjuna fought with Śiva and was also, blessed by Him.

Kālidāsa seems to be a Śaiva. He accepted Rāma as god. The *Raghuvaṁśa* mentioned Rāma in detail. The word *bhakti* has been first found in the *Śvetāśvatara Upaniṣad* which is Śaiva. The *Nārada Bhakti Sūtra* mentions that it has been spoken by Nārada on the directive of Śiva (*idaṁ nārada poktaṁ śivānuśāsanaṁ*).

Relationship of *bhakti* has been assumed with the Āgama rather than the Śruti. Āgama has been defined as the speech or thoughts which had been recited by Śiva, listened by Pārvatī, and is agreeable to Kṛṣṇa.[1] This is a clear reconciliation between Śiva and Kṛṣṇa. Such reconciliation is referred even in the *Rāmacaritamānasa* and *Adhyātma Rāmāyaṇa*. This reconciliation is not made by Tulasīdāsa but earlier. Co-ordination is a specific feature of Indian tradition. All the Smārttas worshipped the five deites. *Ācārya*s of the south assumed the unity of Śiva and Viṣṇu. On the basis of the

1. *āgataṁ śiva vaktrebhyo gataṁ ca girijā śrutau* ।
mataṁ ca vāsudevasya tasmādāgama ucyate ॥
Quoted in Padmacandra and Śrīdhar Bhāsā, *Mānasa Pīyūṣa*, Part 1, p. 38.

Vaiṣṇava Sarvasva, Bharatendu Harishchandra mentioned — Śrī Viṣṇu Svāmī (an *ācārya* of south) was a disciple of Śukadeva Muni . . . Śri Viṣṇu Svāmī along with his maternal uncle Raṅganātha departed for Kāśī for learning but could not reach. He is considered to have been the *ācārya* of Ācārya Vallabha. The same account of Bhāratendu also mentioned that Ācārya Śaṅkara arrived at Kāśī and relinquished the body but was revived. Then he renounced the world and spread *māyāvāda*. In this account there is also a mention of doctrinal debate (*śāstrārtha*) between Sureśvarācārya and Ācārya Śaṅkara that was held in Kāśī.[2] Ancestors of Śrīnātha Jī, the former *ācārya* to Rāmānujācārya, had gone to south from Kāśī. Similarly, Agastya is also assumed to be a resident of Kāśī. He had composed the *Agastyam,* the first grammar in Tamil literature. Rāghavānanda and Rāmānanda also dwelled in Kāśī. Probably, Rāghavānanda had come from south to north. He was the *guru* of Rāmānanda and had come before him. Rāghavānanda is believed to be born in the family of Rāmānuja. He arrived in the north and propagated *Rāma mantra*.[3] Mahāprabhu Vallabhācārya belonged to Tailaṅga region but his parents had come to Kāśī. Ācārya was born on the way. He was initiated in Kāśī.

We have reached to two conclusions yet —

1. There is no conflict between Śiva and Viṣṇu.
2. Basically Kāśī is the city of Śiva. But Vaiṣṇavas also dwelled here respectfully. Kāśī is also that land where Buddha, *avatāra* of Bhagavān Viṣṇu, made his first religious exposition. Selection of Kāśī for his first exposition is an indication of generosity and comprehension.

---

2. *Vaiṣṇava Sarvasva,* Bhāratendu Granthāvalī, pp. 863-68.
3. *vande rāghavācārya rāmānuja kulod bhavāṁyābhyāduttara māgatya rāmamantra pracārakam,* Pitambaradatta Barthwal, *Yoga Pravāha,* p. 2.

Hindi literature is absolutely a Vaiṣṇava literature. The literature from Vidyāpati to Dvivedī era is uncontradictorily Vaisnava. Most of the *chāyāvāda* poets and writers were Vaisnavas. Bharatendu Harishchandra, a promoter of modern Hindi, was also Vaiṣṇava. National poet Maithilisharana Gupta, who first promoted *khaḍī* language poetry, was also Vaiṣṇava. Institutions like Kāśī Vidyāpīṭha, and Banaras Hindu University were under the influence of Vaiṣṇava tradition. Use of non-vegeterian items and wine, etc., were prohibited here. Non-violence had been assumed to be the main base of Vaiṣṇava doctrine. Later, under the influence of Mahatma Gandhi, in the national thought of India, stress was laid on non-violence. So the whole national movement of India should be called a movement under the influence of Vaiṣṇava doctrine. The Vaisnavism of *Śrīmad Bhāgavatam* includes in itself even Buddha and Ṛṣabhadeva. This has given impetus to the spread of Vaisnavism.

Vidyāpati's poetry unites Śiva and Viṣṇu, but there is no such mention which reveals that Vidyāpati had visited any Śaiva or Vaiṣṇava region. In the same way there are many *stotra*s that relate the unity between Hari and Hara. Gorakhanātha lived in Kāśī. Not only the mound (*ṭīlā*) of Gorakhanātha, but also his accounts prove that he was against *pañcamakāra*. Followers of Nātha and Mahānubhāva, in Maharashtra, worship Viṭṭhala. The Vaiṣṇava image of Viṭṭhala is adorned with *Śivaliṅga* on its head. The Gaṅgā, flowing in Kāśī, is the best example of the unity of *Trideva*s (the three gods). Radiance of Kāśī is combined with the simplicity of Viṣṇu and unrestrainness of Śiva. There is absence of conflict between Śiva and Viṣṇu here. This conflict has been mainly perceived in south India. Seeing this conflict in south, a Vaiṣṇava critic of Hindi and a resident of Kāśī, Acharya Rama Chandra Shukla, had derived unity between Śiva and Viṣṇu in the accounts of Tulasīdāsa, although this unity is very old — *vaiṣṇavānāṁ yathā śambhuḥ*. Tulasīdāsa believed in unity among all. Goddess Sītā is that *Ādi Śakti* who creates all. She is Vaiṣṇavī. Dākṣāyaṇī in the *Kāmāyanī* of Prasad is also non-violent. She condemned hunting and sacrifice in *yajña* by Manu. Prasad condemned sacrifice, violence for animals —

> *yajña samāpta ho cuka to bhī dhadhaka rahī thī jwālā* ।
> *dāruṇa dṛśya! rudhira ke chīnṭe asthi khaṇḍa kī mālā* ॥
> *vedī kī nirmama prasannatā paśu kī kātara vāṇī* ।
> *milakara vātāvaraṇa banā thā koī kutsita prāṇī* ॥

Prasad's resistance of violent *yajña* is not new. He who writes poetry on Lord Buddha, is basically of Vaiṣṇava viewpoint. There is a lack of violence in his Śaiva poems too. His accounts are basically literature of non-violence. The *Mahābhārata* also mentions several non-violent *yajña*s. There was a tradition of *yajña*s in *Mahābhārata*. These were performed repeatedly, but there is no mention of animal sacrifice (*paśubali*). Later, the grandeur, expansion of *yajña*s and spirit of victory and defeat stopped with the tradition of *yajña*s. Although Yudhiṣṭhira was non-violent, yet he had performed *Rājasūya yajña* that caused a massive destruction. There is no mention of sacrifice of animals in this *yajña* but Jarāsandha and Śiśupāla were killed for the sake of the *yajña*. Śrī Kṛṣṇa himself did not hunt and sacrifice animals, but he was the main promoter of violence among kings and destruction of kṣatriyas. Mother Gāndhārī blamed him for the war saying that although he could have stopped Mahābhārata war, he stimulated the great war.*

Saint Kabīra was born in Kāśī. He appeared on the lotus leaf in Laharatara pond. This imagery of lotus is related to Viṣṇu. Śiva has no place for lotus. It is believed that Svāmī Rāmānanda, a resident of Panchaganga Ghat, was *guru* of Kabīra. Showing his presence in Kāśī, Kabīra took recourse to

---

* *This is not the correct assessment of Kṛṣṇa's personality. He tried his level best to promote peace and met Duryodhana with a peace proposal. He pardoned hundred abuses of Śiśupāla and did not lift a weapon in the Mahābhārata War. —Editors*

silence about Kāśī. He also took Kāśī as the city of Śiva. Though he lived in Kāśī he did not seem to be a resident of Kāśī. Living in Ayodhyā, Kākabhuśuṇḍi perceived the grandeur of Ayodhyā. Kabīra was different in this context. He wanted to avoid every type of *saguṇa* and *sākāra* (visible). He praised only Rāma not Śiva or so, nor even worldly actions of Rāma. Kabīra selected Magadhagṛha of Magahara for his death. There are two reasons for it — 1. He attached importance to Rāma *bhakti* and not the place, be it Kāśī or any other place,[4] 2. Magadha is the gateway to hell. It is just contrary to Kāśī. He did not want to relinquish his body in an impure region like Magadha. Moreover Kabīra believed in the principle of gaining salvation through Rāma *bhakti*. Saint Garībadāsa said:

> *binā bhagati kā hota hai kāsī karvata leha* ।
> *miṭai nahīn mana vāsanā bahu vidhi bharama sandeha* ॥

Devotees scantify even mud.[5] Kāśī Karavaṭa is too useless without Rāma *bhakti*. There is a place by the name of Karavaṭa in Kāśī. There the people used to tear their bodies with a saw for gaining salvation. Saint Dādū had his learning of Vedānta in Kāśī. Dādū's *maṭha* is embellished at Assi even today. But even Dādū did not describe about Kāśī. Saint Kabīra discussed with Śiva :

> O Śiva! How is your Kāśī? You should yet think about it. There are *covā*, sandal, incense sticks and betel leaf (*pāna*); Smṛtis, Purāṇas are recited at homes, different types of offering are being offered in the palaces; and yet the people of the city are clamouring. You have different types of people. This is what I perceive. I, as a boy, have a little knowledge. What else could be explained to you which came to my mind. Where does a soul go after death? If the soul suffers a loss, it is not the man's fault. It is a matter of shame for the

---

4. *kāsī kāṭai ghara kiyā pīvai nirmala nīra, mukuti nahīn hari nāṅva yauṅ kahai dāsa kabīra* — *Kabīra Samagra*, p. 282.
5. *Bhāgavata* 7.10.19.

> Master (Rāma). Sāhab himself is the Master too. Loss of a *bhakta* is a matter of shame for the Master. Pleased with this Śiva said, "Where I am present, no one can be present there." Have patience for four days.

Kabīra mentions the same which he has seen.[6]

This poem is not vivid but three points are clear — 1. Kabīra assumed Kāśī as the city of Śiva, 2. He has described this city, and 3. He is worried about the salvation of the people of this city. How the voluptuous people of this city could gain salvation? Śiva assured that all of them would gain salvation in four days.

Saint Raidāsa was also a resident of Kāśī. Jhālā Rānī and Mīrabāī belonged to the royal families of Rajasthan. They were disciples of Raidāsa. Raidāsa himself was a disciple of Rāmānanda Svāmī. Situated closed to Kāśī, there is a *maṭha* (residence of a devotee and his disciples), namely, Bhuḍakuḍā in the tradition of *nirguṇa* saints. Many saints belong to this *maṭha*. Generally, the *maṭha*s of all the saints in Kāśī are *upamaṭha*s.

Sometimes, saints used Kaśī as a symbol. Assuming Kāśī as *karma*, Saint Siṅgā held — *karma kī kāsī ecāva jo, khetī cokhī dhāya.*[7] *ghaṭa mein gaṅgā ghaṭa mein jamunā vahī dvārakā kāsī* (Who does the deed pious like Kāśī, he would gain good results.

---

6. *siva kāsī kaise bhaī tohāri, ajahūṅ ho siva dekhu vicāri* ।
cobā candana agara pāna ghara ghara sumriti hoya purāna ।
bahuvidhi bhavananhi lāgu bhoga, nagara kolāhala karata loga ।
bahuvidhi parajā loga tora, tehi kārana cita dīṭha mora ।
hamare balakavā ke ehai gyāna, toharā ke samujhāvai āna ।
je jehi mana se rahala āya, jīva ko marana kahuṅ kahāṅ samāya ।
tākara jo kachu hoya akāla, tāhi, dosa nahin sāhaba lāja ।
hara harakhita soṅ kahala bheva, jahāṅ hama vahāṅ dūsara na keva ।
dinā cāri mana dharahu dhīra, jasa dekhaiṅ tasa kahahin kabiīra ।
— *Kabīr Samagra*, part 1, p. 803

7. *Sant Siṅgā Jī*, ed. Ramanarayana Upadhyaya, p. 86.

Where there is Gaṅgā or Yamunā, that place is pious like Dvārakā and Kāśī.) Garibadasa also assured — *kāyā kāsī chāṇḍi caloge jāya baso mana magharī* (You would have to relinquish the body in Kāśī and dwell in Magharī.) The body is dwelling in Kāśī and the soul in Magahara. Kabīra also said — *kāsī se dhuni upajai kāsī jāī*. Kabīra did not criticise Kāśī rather he assumed it as the region of salvation, but he abandoned Kāśī to establish the significance of Rāma *bhakti* — *carana birada kāsī kūn na raihūn* I *kahai kabīra bhala narakai jaihūn*. If the heart is not filled with simplicity of love, the heart is not modest with the love of God, then a person will go to hell even if he relinquishes his body in Varanasi — *manahu kaṭhora mare banārasa naraka na bāncyā jāī*. Kabīra considered Brahmā, Viṣṇu and Maheśa under delusion (*māyā*). Viṣṇu *loka* (cosmological region) also destroyed — *bisnū loka binase china māhīn*. There is another reason for which Kabīra under-estimated Kāśī. He is *Ādi Puruṣa* (the first man). He is elder to Brahmā, Viṣṇu and Maheśa. Once Gorakhanātha asked him (probably in imagination) — O Kabīra! When did you assume asceticism? Where are you paying your attention?

> *kabīra kaba se bhaye vairāgī tumharī surati kahān ko lāgī?*

Kabīra answered :

> *baicitrā kā melā, nahīn guru nahīn celā* I
> *sakala psārā jisa dina nāhīn, jihi dina puruṣa akelā* II
> *gorakha hama tabake ahain bairāgī* I
> *hamarī surati, brahama son lāgī* II
> *brahmā nahīn jaba ṭopī dīnhī, bisnu nahīn jaba ṭīkā* I
> *siva sakti kai janmau nāhīn, tabai joga hama sīkhā* II
>
> — *Kabīrā Samagra*, p. 765

The man, who existed prior to Brahmā, Viṣṇu, Śiva, Śakti, is connected with Brahma, and if he does not impart significance to the city of Śiva, then it is not a matter of surprise. Kabīra said that he was not born, rather he appeared — *kāsī mein hama pragaṭa bhaye hain*. Kabīra is also *avatāra* like Rāma, Kṛṣṇa, Śiva.

There are two methods to perceive the supreme spirit — *ātma-sādhanā* (self-accomplishment) or *yoga* and *śāstra*. The first method is called *ātamavid* and the second, *śāstravid*. Kabīra was *ātamavid*, whereas Tulasīdāsa *śāstravid*. Both the traditions have been in vogue in Kāśī. Buddha was also *ātmavid*. In the Kṛṣṇa Bhakti literature, Śrī Kṛṣṇa sent Uddhava to *gopīs*. Uddhava advised *gopīs* the path of *nirguṇa, nirākāra, yoga*. He advised them on behalf of Śrī Kṛṣṇa. But *gopīs* did not accept this advice of Śrī Kṛṣṇa. They desired the *sākāra* (visible) form of Śrī Kṛṣṇa. *gopīs* told Uddhava three things :

1. *Yoga* is not the path for women :

   hamare kauna joga vrata sādhai?
   mṛgatvaca bhasma adhāri jaṭā ko ko itanon avarādhai ।

2. Kāśī is the place of *yoga*. So you should take it away to Kāśī, where it would sell on higher prices:

   itanī dūra jāhū calī kāsī jahān bikati hai pyārī ।

3. *Yoga* is unnatural for Braja, it is a heavy load :

   joga moṭa sira bhojha ānī kai kata tuma ghoṣa utārī ।

One can attain the eight supernatural powers (*aṣṭa siddhi*) by *yoga*. These powers are slaves of *gopīs*. Kāśī is the city of Śaṅkara. Accomplishment of *yoga* is suitable only in Kāśī :

joga aṅga sādhata je ūdho te saba basata īsapura kāsī ।

Yoga has been called the art of trickery, which cannot be sold in Braja. We should keep in mind that Sūradāsa was devoted to Śiva first. He was initiated in Vaiṣṇava sect by Ācārya Vallabha. The modern scholars of Kāśī called the message of Uddhava as the message of Kabīra. Sūradāsa was more versed in love than self-versed and *śāstra* versed. Not only knowledge but bestowing gift or dedication is also significant. There is no mention of any visit of Sūradāsa to Kāśī.

Tulasīdāsa came from elsewhere and dwelled in Kāśī. He lived in Bhadaini which is called Tulasi Ghat at present. Earlier, perhaps, it was a Rāma temple. Kabīra was worshipper of that Rāma who dwelt in every heart. He explored Rāma in the very same heart. As a result he became introspective; and remained indifferent to Rāma external, work and pilgrimage. Rāma of Tulasī is present outside more than inside. Tulasīdāsa desired the welfare of mankind. His knowledge being inner seems very beautiful outside — *upajahiṁ ananta anata chavi lahahīṁ*. There are several places, actions and stories related to Tulasīdāsa in Kāśī. He consecrated Hanumān Jī at 12 places. The famous Hanumān temple called Saṅkaṭa Mocana was also probably founded by him. The old name of this temple was Bāga Gosāi Tulasīdāsa Jī Bākā Mosūmā Saṅkaṭa Mocana. The tradition of *Rāmalīlā* was also initiated by Tulasīdāsa. Perhaps Meghā Bhagata who is believed to have begun the *Rāmalīlā* was a disciple of Tulasīdāsa. These *Rāmalīlā*s were played on the basis of the *Rāmacaritmānasa.* Prior to this, the basis of *Rāmalīlā* was perhaps the Vālmīki's *Rāmāyaṇa.* Tulasīdāsa founded *Kṛṣṇalīlā*s too at several places, which are in vogue even these days. The basis of *Kṛṣṇalīla* is the tenth section of the *Bhāgavata.* These *līlā*s are performed from the 13th day of the dark half to the 13th day of the bright half of the month of Āśvina. Tulasīdāsa was also deeply attached to the Mṛtyuñjaya Mahādeva temple, Gopāla temple, Hanumān Phāṭaka, etc.

One narration mentions that Tulasīdāsa composed the *Rāmacaritmānasa* in *bhākhā* on the order of Bhagavān Viśvanātha. There are two narrations which recognize the *Rāmacaritmānasa*.

1. First of all, the famous philosopher Madhusūdana Sarasvatī recognized *Mānasa*.
2. Secondly, Śaṅkarajī Himself recognized *Mānasa*.

There is no sign of the presence of Śrī Rāma in Kāśī, then also. Even if Tulasīdāsa mentioned the significance of Kāśī in most of his literature, he gave more importance to Kāśī than Ayodhyā, the birthplace of Rāma. It is so because Śaṅkara and Pārvatī dwelled in Kāśī :

mukti janma mahi jāni gyāna khāni aga hāni kara ।
jahaṁ basa saṁbhu bhavāni so kāsī seia kasa na ॥
— *Rāmacaritamānasa*, 4

There are four characteristics of Kāśī — 1. bestowing salvation, 2. abundance of knowledge, 3. remover of sins, and 4. dwelling of Śambhu and Bhavānī. The aforesaid couplet reveals that Tulasīdāsa was devoted to Śiva more than to Rāma. In Ayodhyā he was concerned only with Sītā-Rāma while in Kāśī he found Śiva in three forms — servant, master and friend of Rāma. While Rāma worships Ayodhyā, Tulasīdasa's focus was on Kāśī. Kāśī has nothing to do with Rāma, but only with the devotees of Rāma or Rāma *bhakta*. In this very place he established one of Śaṅkara's *avatāra*, Sankar Suvana Hanumān Jī. Kāśī is situated just on Magadha, on the banks of the Gaṅgā. The Karmanāśā (destroyer of deeds) is present in Magahara and the Gaṅgā in Kāśī. Both the rivers give opposite results. To escape from confusion it is said that Śiva always recites *mahāmantra* of Rāma *nāma*. He preached that the salvation was possible in Kāśī :

mahāmantra joi japata mahesū, kāsī mukuti hetu upadesū ।

Kāśī is significant for two reasons — 1. uninterrupted utterance (*japa*) of the name of Rāma by Śaṅkara, 2. exhortation of salvation by Śaṅkara. If he did not utter the name of Rāma then he could not make the exhortation of salvation. For the cause of utterance of Rāma *nāma*, Śiva is *guru* too. There are several Vaiṣṇava places like Panchapandava, Kapiladhara in Kāśī itself. For the cause of *Rāmalīlās* there are several sectors in Kāśī related to *Rāmakathā*, like, Avadhgarvi, Lanka, etc. The liberal God bestows salvation and adoration even to the insects and grasshoppers of Kāśī (Purāripur) :

veda vidita tehi pada purāri pura kīta pataṅga samāhīṁ ı

Śaṅkara is the Head of the gods of Kāśī hence known as Mahādeva. He dwells in the crematorium of Kāśī. Tulasīdāsa requested Hanumān for bestowing the boon for appearance of Rāma in Kāśī. Hanumān got Rāma appear before him. In Kāśī itself Tulasīdāsa begs Śiva for grace of Śrī Rāma :

dehi kāmāri śrī rāma pada pankaje ı
bhakti manavarata gatabheda māyā ıı
— *Vinaya*

In the *Vinaya Patrikā,* Tulasīdāsa beseeches adoration and salvation from all Gods and Goddesses dwelling in Kāśī. After Śiva he prays to Pārvatī and Gaṅgā. After the *Mānasa,* the *Vinaya Patrikā* is the most significant work of Tulasīdāsa. It is a request for mercy submitted to the royal court of Rāma. So it consists of prayers to Rāma, Sītā and the whole Rāma family. Apart from one *pada* for Yamunā and two *pada*s for Citrakūṭa, it expounds the significance of Kāśī. Of the two latter *pada*s, one is for Kāśī itself. It is also a description of the geographical situation of Kāśī. Kāśī is *Kāmadhenu* too, *kalikāmadhenu kāsī.* In the *Dohāvalī,* there are two couplets which mention the circumstances of Kāśī — Robbers are wandering throughout the day, thieves in the night. "O Śaṅkara! Please save your city. O Śiva it is your *Bīsī* (destroying position of the planets). Only you can save us from it."[8]

He mentioned in the *Uttara Kāṇḍa* of *Kavitāvalī* — Śiva and Pārvatī are the owners of Kāśī. The attendants of Rudra (*Rudragaṇa*) are warriors. Kārttikeya, the leader of ghosts, (*Bhūta Gaṇapati*) is the Army Chief. But they are not driving away the fearful form of Kālī. The situation of the city is pathetic due to *Bīsī.* In the *Loka Veda*s Kāśī has been praised.

8. *bāsa ḍhāsani ke ḍhakā rajanī cahuṅ disi cora, saṅkara nija pura rākhiye citai sulocana kora. do* ıı 239 ıı

apanī bīsīṅ āpuhiṅ purihiṅ lagāe hātha, kehi vidhi binatī bisva kā karauṅ bisva ke nātha ıı 240 ıı

The men and women of Kāśī are similar to Śiva and Pārvatī respectively. Kālanātha himself is the *kotavāla*. Bhairava is *Daṇḍapāṇi* (magistrate). Śaṅkara is the king. Even knowing so, Kalikāla is encouraging wicked conduct. Mischievous people are flourishing while the virtuous are suffering from distress. Innocent persons are being punished and the criminals are enjoying. O Śiva! You had established *pañcakosa* as the region of auspicious deeds and bestowed everyone with abode. But those men and women could not sustain the honour given by you. They joined in wicked deeds. Epidemic is the result of the same. Śrī Kṛṣṇa had set Varanasi on fire, but he was afraid of you. Epidemic is due to your resentment, yet we rely on you. You had drunk the *kālakūṭa* (poision) for the welfare of the world. There is a mention of rise and fall of circumstances of Kāśī in the *Uttara Kāṇḍa, chanda* 169 to 183. Tulasīdāsa has not described any other city as much as Kāśī. Tulasīdāsa also mentioned the grandeur of the people of Kāśī, but he is distressed by their conducts. He prayed for reform in the conduct of the people of Kāśī and also for the mercy of God. Any reform can take place only with the grace of God. To attain the blessings of God we have to improve ourselves.

According to Pandita Kuberanatha Shukla, the author of the *Vārāṇasī Vaibhava*, at first the region of Kāśī was a pilgrimage of Viṣṇu. Later it got converted into Śiva pilgrimage. It has been mentioned in the two Purāṇas — *Nārada Purāṇa* and *Vāmana Purāṇa*. *Śloka* of *Nārada Purāṇa* is as under :

ādyaṁ ca vaiṣṇavaṁ sthānaṁ purāṇe paricakṣate ।
purīṣu saṁsthito viṣṇuraṁśaiḥ kāśyāṁ svarūpataḥ ।
kāśī svarūpa viṣṇostu yatra sākṣāt prakāśate ।

6

Vaiṣṇava Ideology of Kabīra

Shyam Sundara Shukla

It is impossible to determine what were the real principles for accomplishment, that Kabīra had adopted. He extracted the essence of different conducts and views (manners of life). He felt no hesitation in accepting those contemporary conducts and views which he considered appropriate, suitable to place and time and related to the welfare of all. He abandoned those views firmly that were insubstantial or non-acceptable from his viewpoint. On the basis of those conclusions which have been drawn from different sources, evidences and beliefs available about his ideology, it can be said firmly that he was very much influenced by the Vaiṣṇava ideology of Vaiṣṇava Ācārya Svāmī Rāmānanda, an epoch-making saint in those times. It is quite natural also as he was brought up in Kāśī and had spent most of his life there. It is believed that Svāmī Rāmānanda had twelve disciples in all who were followers of *saguṇa* and *nirguṇa* paths. Kabīra was held best of all among those disciples who have been considered as *nirguṇa bhakta*s (followers of the formless).[1] A list of those disciples has been found as under —

---

1. Pt. Baldev Prasad Upadhyaya, *Bhāgavata Sampradāya*, p. 519.

   (i) Disciples combined with "Ānanda" Āspada — Anantānanda, Sursurānanda, Narharyyānanda, Yogānanda, Sukhānanda, Bhavānanda and Gālavānanda.

→

śrīmadanantānandastu surasurānandastathā ।
narahariyānandastu yogānandastathaiva ca ॥
sukhā bhavāgālavaśca saptaite nāma nandanāḥ ।
kabīraśca rabīdāsaḥ senā pīpādhanastathā ।
padmāvatī tadarddhaśca ṣaḍete ca jitendriyāḥ.[2]

Svāmī Rāmānanda (fourteenth century) has a particular place and a significance in the history of tradition of Vaiṣṇava *ācārya*s of northern India. Living in Kāśī he diffused religious devotion directed towards the Supreme Being seen as positively personal, external and internal (mental) accomplishment system and philosophical ideology of progressive Viśiṣṭādvaita (qualified non-duality) all over India. He named *Brahma* as Rāma and expounded both the practice of adoration — *nirguṇa* and *saguṇa*. The aforesaid *śloka* also confirms that among the disciples of Svāmī Rāmānanda, seven were followers of *saguṇa* who had assumed the title of *ānanda*, whereas the other five disciples along with Padmāvatī (among whom Kabīra was incomparable) were followers of the *nirguṇa* path.

In the *Rāmavata Sampradāya*, expounded by Svāmī Rāmānanda, Rāma along with Sitā is worthy of adoration. In the field of accomplishment and adoration the difference concerning sex, caste and creed, and religion and community is meaningless. Earlier restrictions related to conduct were also mostly denounced. He adopted the same path of devotion which was already expounded in the *Bhaktisūtras* of Śāṇḍilya and Nārada and supported by the *Śrīmad Bhāgavata*. He spread the knowledge, asceticism and devotion in a combined form. His *nirguṇa* ideology combined with devotion of Rāma also attracted the male and female ascetics of the castes other than brāhmaṇas. Although Kabīra assumed the formless Rāma as

→ (ii) *Jitendriya* (whose senses or passions are subdued) saints — Kabīra, Raidās, Senā, Pīpā, Dhannā and Padmāvatī (who is assumed half in counting)

2. *Kabīra Granthāvalī*, *pada* 124.

worthy of his adoration and followed the five rites like drawing of impression (*mudrāṅkana*), holding of vertical *puṇḍra*, naming, reciting of *mantra*s and holding of garland made with sacred basil plant, yet he assumed with entirety and spread the principles that preached devoted love for God, uninterrupted meditation on the name Rāma, *prapatti*, *bhagavat-kaiṅkarya*, acquiring good tendencies and abandoning the bad ones.

Thus we find that Saint Kabīra adheres to the principles of Svāmī Rāmānanda in meditation as well as in the customary behaviour. In compliance with his *guru*'s directions, Kabīra adopted the means of melodious adoration, accepted the devotional accomplishment free from the customs of Śāstras, encouraged the vision of equanimity and co-ordination, and adhered to the qualified non-dual philosophy of Nāmapaṅthī ideology. It is the same path of devotion that is indicated in the scripture, *Siddhānta Pañcamātrā* composed by Svāmī Rāghavācārya (Rāmānanda's *guru*) and interpreted and explained by the scripture *Vaiṣṇvamatābja Bhāskara* of Svāmī Rāmānanda.

On the other hand, Kabīra's beliefs relating to conduct and views of accomplishment also appear to be influenced by the Kṛṣna-*bhakta* poets of Maharashtra who were influenced by Nāyanār and Āḷvār *bhakta*s of south India. Maharashtra was deeply influenced by Śrī Śaṭhakopācārya, Kureśa Svāmī, Lokācārya, Andāla and Bakhara Muni, etc., of south in those times. Therefore, northern India was very much influenced by Saint Kabīra's predecessor and contemporary saints like Śrī Bhānudāsa Mahārāja, Saint Ekanātha, Ananta Mahārāja, Tukārāma, Kānhobā (younger brother of Tukārāma), Bahiṇā Bāī (disciple of Tukārāma), Keśava Svāmī, Amṛta Rāma, Kṛṣṇa Dāsa, Devanātha, Gulāba Mahārāja, Māṇika, etc., Saint Nāmadeva diffused the same Vaiṣṇava vision in west-north India apart from Maharashtra which was spread by Kabīra in his own manner.

Śrī Kṛṣṇa was worshipped by the name of Śrī Viṭṭhala in Bārkarī sect of Saint Nāmadeva. Method of accomplishment (*sādhanā*) and adoration (*upāsanā*) was in the combined form of *saguṇa* and *nirguṇa* in the same sect. The followers and promulgators of this sect included the Gorā Kumhāra, Sāṁvatā Mālī, Saint Cokhāmelā, Janābāī, Narahari Sunāra, Senānāī, and many other saints of those times from Maharashtra and its neighbouring states and Kāśī was a pilgrimage for them. Therefore, the process of exchange of the views relating to accomplishment was in progress. All of these saints made continuous efforts to make their individual accomplishments applicable to the welfare of entire humanity. Their spiritual instructions were aimed at the diffusion of humanitarian and harmonious vision and ethics in the disorganized society. It was basically aimed at creation of an atmosphere for unanimity, harmony and spiritual unity. Therefore, to credit the Vaiṣṇava sects for the awareness of Hindus would be absolutely right.

In the *dalit*s (supressed) or those other than the *savarṇa* castes, the awareness of self-respect and eradication of their communal inferiority complex is also a legacy of the same *bhakta*s. As a result the saints like Nāmadeva, Kabīra, Raidāsa and Sena have mentioned their caste proudly and have not tried to hide it. Kabīra called himself *korī* or *julāhā* without any hesitation. He said proudly :

jāti julāhā mati ko dhīra । *haraṣi haraṣi guṇa ramai kabīra* ॥[3]
x x x x x x x
tu bābhana main kāsī kā julāhā būjhahū mora giyānā ।
x x x x x x x
mere rāma kī abhaipada nagarī kahai kabīra julāhā ॥
x x x x
julāhai tani buni pāra na pāvala ।
x x x x
korī ko kāhū marama na jānā,[4]

3. *Kabīra Vacanāvalī* — *Rāga Dhanāśrī*, p. 55 (*pada* 58).
4. *Kabīra Granthāvalī*, p. 82.

His argument is :

eka būṅda ekai mala mūtara, eka cāma eka gūdā ।
eka joti se saba jaga utpanā, kauna bābhana kauna sūdā ।[5]

Kabīra said that the people who deride his caste should not forget that in the same caste such a person has taken birth who is a true *bhakta* of God.[6] On the contrary he asked the proud brāhmaṇas and Turks with which cause they are different from him? He asked brāhmaṇa —

je tūṅ bābhana bābhanī jāyā । *tau āna bāṭa hvai kāhe na āyā?*

Similarly he asked Turk —

je tūṅ turaka turakanī jāyā । *bhītara khatanā kyoṅ na karāyā?*

What is meant here is that the leadership of saint Kabīra, the follower of the formless worship (*nirguṇa bhakti*), had made collective efforts for reawakening in the social, cultural and religious aspects, whose influence is present even today. As a result the *akhāḍās* (place of assembly of *sādhus*) belong to the followers of Śaiva and Vaiṣṇava, and there is a majority and domination of *savarṇas*. When Śrī Rāma, the saviour of *gīdha, vyādha* and Śabarī, did not make any communal distinction, and gave importance only to emotions, then his devotees should also not behave inversely. It implies that in the establishment of communal love the contribution of Rāma *Bhakta* poets like Kabīra is very precious. Indicating the same fact Nābhādāsa, composer of *Bhaktamāla* and belonging to the Rāmānandī disciples tradition, has rightly said about Kabīra —

---

5. *kabīra merī jāti kau, sabhu hoi hansanehāru* ॥
balihārī is jāti kau, jihi japiyo sirajana hāru ।
— *Kabīra Granthāvalī*, p. 164

6. *Bhaktamāla* (Nābhādāsa), *Chappaya* 60.

kabīra kāni rākhī nahin baranāśrama ṣaṭ darasanī ।
bhakti vimukha je dharama tāhi adharama kari gāyo ।
joga jagya japa dāna bhajana binu tuccha dikhāyo ॥[7]

The aforesaid lines clearly state that saint Kabīra was against those paths which were against *bhakti* and which led to hypocritical accomplishment. In his view the *haṭha-yogī*s, Śāktas, Śaivas and *tāntrika*s were the sects who adopted such paths of accomplishment. Among these he was a firm opponent of Śāktas. His following compositions could be quoted as an example —

sākhata bābhana nā mile, vaiṣṇo mile caṇḍāla ।
aṅkamāla dai bheṅṭiye, māno mile gopāla ॥
athavā
vaiṣṇoṅ kī chaparī bhalī, nā sākhata baḍa gāṅva ।
candana kī kuṭakī bhalī, na babūra aṁbarāun ॥

Vaiṣṇava Devotion and Kabīra

Kabīra's devotion to Rāma was not motivated by any sort of selfishness; rather it aimed only at the welfare of the people. Not only this, his devotion was not related even to the desire of enjoyment and salvation. What he only desired was that his adored Śrī Rāma should take away the distress of the creatures. All the nine types of devotion, which have been called *navadhā bhakti*, are included more or less in the devotion of Kabīra. Even the beliefs about *pīra-auliyā*, etc., are included in it. The followers of other sects or paths have been limited to any one type of devotion but the devotion of Kabīra is so variegated that it becomes unique. Indicating to this aspect he has himself said :

sataguru ho mahārāja sāī mo pai raṅga ḍārā ।
surajana munijana pīra auliyā, koi na pāvaipārā ॥

---

7. Shyamsundar Shukla, *Hindī Kāvya Kī Nirguṇa Dhārā Mein Bhakti*, pp. 48-84.

sāhaba kabīra sarva raṅga raṅgiyā ।
saba raṅga te raṅga nyārā ॥

Knowledge and *yoga* are assisting elements to this devotion. Restraint, righteousness, restraining the breath, *ajapā-japa* (name of deity as per breath), notion, meditation, *samādhi* (profound meditation with the mind successfully fixed upon the Ultimate Being) and the other forms of *yoga* help to keep the body and mind healthy and under control. As a result, a healthy man often has a virtuous conduct. So the utterances related to *yoga* in the *vāṇī*s of saint Kabīra are the means of assessing the nature of his devotion.

Although the devotion of Kabīra was based on love, it was different from *saguṇa* and *nirguṇa* devotion approved by Svāmī Rāmānanda. While the dual natured devotion (*dvividhā bhakti*) of Svāmī Rāmānanda was based on knowledge gained from Vedas, Purāṇas and learning or meditative knowledge, the devotion of Kabīra was incited by his own feeling and mysticism. He believed that those people cannot adopt the devotion combined with love, who spoke elaborately about the knowledge gained from books and who are egoist on the basis of caste, money, position and power. He felt that it was simply impossible for the lascivious, hot-tempered and greedy persons to devote to *bhakti*. *Bhakti* was meant for those people who were courteous, integrating, abandoning, religious and not hypocrite, and have a feeling of self-dedication to such an extent that they could openly say :

main gulāma mohin beṅci gusāīn । *tana mana dhana mera rāma jī kī tāīn* ॥
becai rāma to rākhai kauna । *rākhai rāma to bechai kauna* ॥

or

kabīra kūtā rāma kā, mutiyā mero nāuṅ ।
gale prema kī jeṅvaḍī, jita khaiṅce tita jāuṅ ॥
tū tū karai to bāhudauṅ, dura dura kahai ta jāuṅ ॥
jyoṅ rākhai taisaiṅ rahauṅ, becai to bika jāuṅ ॥

Humbleness is necessary for devotion. It is the opponent of ego and one of the principal characteristic of devotion. Kabīra himself is of this nature and expects the very same from others too. He said :

> *roḍā hvai rahu bāṭa kā, taji pākhaṇḍa abhimāna* ।
>
> . . . .
>
> *kabīra cerā santa kā, dāsana kā paradāsa* ।
> *kabīra ese hvai rahā, jyon pāuṅ tara ghāsa* ।

In this manner, the students of Kabīra literature would find an appeal made at different places in his *vaṇi*s to adopt the divine virtues and abdicate dubious conduct. The following are the virtues and the vices, laid down by the *Śrimad Bhagvad Gītā*, that are ought to be adopted and abdicated respectively.

Divine virtues mentioned in Gītā — (1) fearlessness, (2) purity of inner heart, (3) firmness in knowledge, (4) firmness in meditation and *yoga*, (5) donation, (6) suppression of senses, (7) worship of God and elders, (8) practice of virtuous deeds, (9) glorifying the virtues and names of God, (10) association with the good people, (11) non-violence, (12) truth, (13) devoid of anger, (14) sacrifice, (15) peace, (16) abdication of pride on accomplishment, (17) lack of volatility, (18) not to criticize anyone, (19) compassion for all creatures, (20) detachment to sensual enjoyment, (21) placid-humbleness, (22) conduct against social-behaviourism, (23) sense of decency, (24) inconstancy, (25) splendour, (26) forgiveness, (27) steadfastness, (28) vitality, (29) purity of body and mind, (30) free from opposing temperament, (31) abdication of treachery, (32) having pure and simple food, (33) worship of scholars, (34) physical penance with purity, simplicity, asceticism.

Demon tendencies — (1) pretence, (2) pride, (3) anger, (4) hardness, (5) stupidity, (6) impurity, (7) untrue conduct, (8) believing the world Godless, (9) belief in passionate world, (10) cruelty, (11) lustfulness, (12) arrogance, (13) haughty,

(14) corrupt conduct, (15) devoured by innumerable anxieties, (16) engrossed in earthly enjoyment, (17) strongly clutched by greed and desires, (18) engrossed in passion, (19) collection of money, etc., in unjust manner, (20) untrue vow, (21) prone to illusion, (22) frenzied in lust of money-honour-post, etc., (23) aversion to each other and thoughtful of having more or less, and (24) impure food-habit.

Assisting elements of devotion

*Bhakta*s of God believed that the accomplishment of devotion is impossible without reverential belief, faith, submission to deity, good company, guidance of a *guru*, calm and secluded meditation, subduing of desires, service to holymen, rendering absolute dedicated love, knowledge, asceticism, forebearance and disinterest. A firm reverence to *guru* and holy men is an essential prerequisite for gaining the highest ascent of devotion. At the same time *saguṇa, sākāra* and *sopādhi* reverence should also be maintained towards the adored, because the beloved one cannot be formless. Apprised of this experience Kabīra meditated upon his endeared Śrī Rāma in various titles each expressing the attitude of *saguṇa*, like Govinda, *dātā*, source of nectar, lover, *ṭhākura*, omniscient, all-pervading, Gopāla, Giridhara and many others.

Zeal of love of such an affectionate *bhakta* combined with the virtues like desire of non-return, growing every time, uninterrupted, rich in self-feelings are beyond description just like a dumb's distinction of flavour. Such a lover gets totally absorbed in his deity as the salt get immersed in water. It implies that both become identical. Supporting this fact Bhakta Nābhādāsa has also said —

> *bhakti bhakta bhagavanta guru, catura nāma bapu eka,*
> *inake pada vandana kiye, kāṅṭein vighana aneka.*

It implies that the devotion, devotee, God and *guru* — all the four are one single element and they vary minutely.

Sant Kabīra's absorption in his God is as deep as between a lover and beloved, and husband and wife. There is no concealment or secrecy in it. Kabīra has himself accepted that *hari mere pīva main rāma kī bahuriyā* (Hari is my husband and I am wife of Rāma) or *dulahini gāvahu maṅgalācāra, hama ghara āye rājā rāma bhatāra* or *hari mero pīva māī hari mero pīva, una bina rahi na sakai mero jīva*. Thus, he is not only the married wife of Rāma but also his *dāsī* (female slave), *cerī* (disciple) and mistress too. But this deep relation was established only after the firmness of *prema bhakti* (devotion combined with love) or such notion as between a couple. At the initial stage of devotion Kabīra called his adored Rāma mother, father, *gosāīn* (owner), protector and guardian. But it is a fact that no notion can touch the height of Kabīra's feeling of anguish of separation and the depth of its expression. His accomplishment of anguish of separation is incomparable.

What can be said about the mysterious personality of Sant Kabīra Sāhib is that as *jākī rahī bhāvnā jaisī, hari mūrata dekhī tina taisī* (one see the image of God as one perceives) he was a follower of action (*karma*) or knowledge or devotion. This question is complex in itself because the nature and character of his beliefs relating to meditative accomplishment is also not absolutely clear. Some called him mysterious while others held him social reformer or religious leader. An evident illustration of the process and experience of accomplishment of *yoga*, and also references to pulse (*nāḍī*), curve (*cakra*), *surati-nirati, brahmarandhra*, in the literature of Kabīra are obstructive in considering him as a pure *bhakta*. Yet the mention of love and the secrets in the relation of husband-wife, servant-owner, father-son, etc., in his compositions are ample proof for placing him in the category of *saguṇa bhakta*.

Kabīra is a product of the newly emerged diffused tradition all around him. His contribution to India in the fifteenth century still holds significance. He was born and brought up and also worked in the devotional atmosphere of

Kāśī. In those days the wave of devotion had overpowered the Bauddha, Jaina, Nāthpantha, Bārkarī, Sūfī and other religious sects. Basically, this devotion was gifted by Nāyanārs (devotees of Śiva) and Āḷvārs (devotees of Viṣṇu) of south India and partly diffused by Rāmānuja in north India, but Kabīra credited his Guru Rāmānanda for it. Later, with the development of Vaiṣṇava accomplishment, devotion (*bhakti*) came to be considered best in all the paths of accomplishment by virtue of its accessibility, simplicity, easy understanding and many other qualities. Thus, along with Kabīra the *bhakta* poets of Hindi are just links of the Indian devotional tradition. In experience they are cent per cent *bhakta* of Indian tradition, even if their manifestation seems to be influenced by the Islamic Sūfīs and Nātha sects.[8]

Devotion of Kabīra, like those of the Jainas and Vaiṣṇavas, emphasizes on the purity of conduct. Sant Kabīra was a living link between the Nātha tradition and most of the sects of those times which were against the accomplishment of *saguṇa.* He has advocated the need of self-knowledge, repressing of desires, notion of valour in devotion, prevention of depraved knowledge, and has also defined the form of *nirguṇa Brahman,* feeling of direct love towards Him. He has expounded the significance of *guru,* support to *karmavāda* and rebirth, the significance of good conduct, criticism of the hypocrites, co-ordination between words and action, imagination of gaining Nirañjana (God) in void, free from physical disease, faith in *yoga* practices, tendency of remaining aloof from debate, refutation of image-worship, aversion to inequalities of castes, suspicion to fast, pilgrimage and worship supported by the Vaidhī tradition, sermon on *bhakti-bhajana* (devotion-devotional song) expounding the significance of *satsaṅga* (association with virtuous people), prevention of criticism of

---

8. *kabīra rekha sindūra kī, kājala diyā na jāya* ।
nainu ramaiyā rami rahyā, dūjā kahāṅ samāya ॥ — *Kabīra, pada* 175

woman, and killing of creatures, criticism of untruth, proclamation of subtle Veda, etc. It was so advocated because in the cultural atmosphere of that era the very same conduct and views had been relevant. Realizing the same need Vaiṣṇava Ācārya Svāmī Rāmānanda thus adopted the same views and possessed the authority of a *guru* (post of *guru*) of the *bhakta*s like Kabīra.

Influence of Sūfism on the Devotional-accomplishment of Kabīra

Though Kabīra had to compete with Sūfīs when he took the resolve to spread his spiritual endeavour for pretensionless devotional accomplishment, ultimately he succeeded in influencing the Sūfī saints like Śekhatakī, Akaradī, Sakardī, etc., to perceive that the following stages of Sūfī *sadhanā* were also included in his accomplishment — (1) sharp (keen) eagerness or curiosity for searching out the truth, (2) search of *Guru* and after finding him receiving religious instructions zealously, (3) stage of spiritual vigil, (4) stage of conscience and asceticism, (5) stage of self-purification (adorning) and emotionality, (6) stage of some perception (relation), (7) struggle with hurdles on the way of accomplishment, (8) anguish of separation, (9) stage of entrusting (surrendering), (10) pre-stage of meeting, (11) stage of pleasure after the meeting, (12) absolute self-surrender or submission, (13) stage of sameness. In Sūfī terminology these should be considered as included under — (1) *sharīyata* (*tau'bā, riyāẓ, khauf* (fear), *muhabbat* (love), etc. (2) *tarīkata* (pre-stage of attainment), (3) *māriphata* (feeling), and (4) *hakīkata* (stage of knowledge). In the Indian worship system, these four steps signify *karma-kāṇḍa* (religious rites), adoration, knowledge and *nirvāṇa*.

Although in ascertaining the form of *prema-bhakti* or *premā-bhakti* (devotion of love) of Kabīra, the influence of Sūfī *prema sādhanā* appeared clear, nonetheless it can be said that he had his own vision and he accepted any view only when it conformed to this vision. Not considering the entire form of his accomplishment if we take into account his *prema sādhanā* only, then we perceive that in this field he was neither wholly influenced by the Vaiṣṇava nor by the Sūfī's ideology. Hence, Kabīra's expression of feeling of love seems somewhat different from the used Indian standard of expression of love. While the Indian *prema-sādhanā* is imbued with tenderly feeling (*mādhurya*), Kabīra's *sādhanā* is full of frenzy. While the Indian love has remained restrained to dignity, the love of Kabīra is explicit like the love of a mature woman. His love is supporter of enjoying freely abounding the regards for public opinion. There is no space for shyness and duality in it.[9]

In the aforesaid chain there are yet some more differences between the Indian and Sūfī's feeling and expression of love. The former is imbued with restraint and contentment whereas the latter lacks both the elements. The former has the capacity to assimilate everything whereas the latter seems eager to express everything. While the former wish for kind glance and vicinity of his supreme lover the latter sees the gleam of delight in the suffering of love. The former desperately desire to meet his lover while the latter perceive the meaning of life in the suffering or anguish of separation. One perceives his lover in the open space of nature whereas the other closes his eyes from the visible world after enclosing his supreme lover within his eyes. The love in the case of the former is humble and kind whereas in the latter it is exciting and frenzied. In the former case the supreme lover is the single man of the world and the rest of the men-women are similar to his wives whereas the latter considered his lover like such woman who is the controlling principle and is the centre of attraction for the entire world. Despite these differences the Indian and Sūfī love exhibit similarity as they both aim at gaining their lover.

---

9. Jāyasī, *Granthāvalī* (preface), p. 146.

Not only the saints of *Jñānamārgī* sect were influenced by the ideology and expression genre of sūfīs, even the Kṛṣṇa-bhakti sect was more or less influenced. From this viewpoint the following statement of Ācārya Rāmacandra Śukla attracts attention :

> Besides Mīrā, some more Kṛṣṇa *bhakta*s were also fully influenced by the Sūfīs. The tendencies of Sūfīs are well seen reflected in the ideology of Caitanya Mahāprabhu. Just as Sūfī *kauwwāl*s soon attain the state of *hāla* while singing, in the same way the *bhakta*s group of Mahāprabhu also used to become unconscious during singing and dancing. Similarly, *mada* (frenzy), *pyālā* (cup), *unmāda* (madness) and lover are the suggested expression of God which are fixed tendencies of Sūfīs and which have been followed by some subsequent Kṛṣṇa *bhakta* poets. Nāgarīdās Jī swayed continuously after taking "Cup of love" (immersing in frenzy of love). . . . In the tradition of the *nirguṇa* sects, though the saints like Kabīra, Dādū, etc., have the knowledge of Indian Vedānta, their love is absolutely similar to the love of Sūfīs. Among those Dādū, Dariyā Sāhab, etc., seem purely Sūfī.[10]

Contrary to the aforesaid notion of Ācārya Rāmacandra Śukla Dr. Hajārīprasād Dvivedī holds the opinion :

> If we take into account the surface meaning of the speeches (*vāṇīs*) of *nirguṇavādī* saints like Kabīra then it will appear that it is absolutely Indian and it has direct connection with the *pada*s of the latter *siddha*s of the Bauddha *dharma* and *yogī*s of Nāthapanthī . . . whether in language, emotion, rhetoric (*alaṅkāra*), metre, or terminology — all are to the guides of Kabīradās.[11]

In this context Dvivedī Jī also argued that :

> Even if the saint poets like Kabīra have taken the essence of love from the Sūfī *sādhanā* they have assimilated it such that

---

10. *Hindi Sāhitya Kī Bhūmikā*, p. 31.
11. *Ibid.*, p. 37.

it had lost its original form. Just as his Rāma was not the son of Daśaratha even though taken from Vaiṣṇava Śāstras, in the same way his *sahaja* (easy), *śūnya* (void), *ṣaṭacakra* (six rings), *iḍā*, *piṅgalā*, etc., also differed in meaning from that of *sahajayāna* and *yogīs*. Not only this, they had even arranged those words in their own way which were taken from the Sūfī *sādhanā*.[12]

Vaiṣṇava Influence on Notion of Devotion of Kabīra

The influence of Vaiṣṇava adoration was more strong than the Sūfī adoration and thoughts in the field of meditation. There was a clear clash between the *saguṇa* worship and Kabīra's *nirguṇa* worship. But the difference that appeared between the two was only external because their basic element was the same. Even Kabīra had never evaluated himself less than any Vaiṣṇava. Kabīra's devotion has been called as *jñāna bhakti* (devotion with knowledge), *surati mein nirati*, *sahajā bhakti* (easy devotion), and *nāradī bhakti*! In short, this devotion is a distinctive edition of Vaiṣṇava devotion.

In the *saguṇa* Vaiṣṇava adoration, *nirguṇa* is worshipped in *saguṇa* whereas Kabīra was a worshipper of *saguṇa* in *nirguṇa*. Even if called wise, Kabīra was not a mere wise man but also a worshipper and similarly, a Vaiṣṇava *bhakta* is not a mere *bhakta* or worshipper. Hence, both are partly the follower of the path of knowledge and worship as well. Though called as *brahmavādī*, Kabīra was a worshipper of Rāma, Hari, Kamalāpati, Nārāyaṇa, Murāri, Keśava, Mādhava, Jagannātha, Śārṅgapāṇi, Kṛṣṇa, Gopāla, Govinda, etc. Vaiṣṇava sect on the other hand, is still *brahmavādī* even though it is called the worshipper of Rāma and Kṛṣṇa. So it is clear that it would not be appropriate to consider Kabīra as belonging to *jñānāśrayī*

---

12. *jñāna dhūpa mana puṣpa indriya hutāśanam* ।
chimā jāpa samādhi pūjā namo deva nirañjanam ॥
— *Rāmānanda Kī Hindī Racanāyen*, p. 3 *pada* 2

branch apart from *saguṇa* worshipper, assuming him a wise man (*jñānī*).

As said earlier, Kabīra was fully influenced by Rāmānanda. So far as the questions of belief in the *piṇḍastha* a (spirit in human body), internal adoration of Nātha Nirañjana (title of the Ultimate Being), *yoga sādhanā* (practice of meditation), *ajapājapa* (silent prayer of the self-existent deity,[13] *Brahman*), *unmanī* and *khecarī*, practice of postures like Bhūcarī, etc., description of *nāda-bindu* and *suratinagara-varṇana*, splinter of love, *jñānaviraha* (suffering of separation along with knowledge),[14] *akhaṇḍa jyotidarśana* (observance of ever burning light) and *surati-nirati-saṅgama* are concerned, Kabīra certainly acquired guidance from the religious instructions of Svāmī Rāmānanda. The book *Rāmānanda Kī Hindī Racanāeṅ* published by the Nāgarī Pracāriṇī Sabhā may be mentioned as an evidence. From this we can even draw a conclusion that this scripture has also been the source of thoughts of Kabīra. Furthermore, the scripture may even help in resolving any complication or controversy that may arise in expounding the doctrinal *sūtra*s and different types of thoughts and utterances related to different principles which may seem like paradox available in the literature of Kabīrā. After learning the following lines of Śrī Rāmānanda who could say that for description of the feelings of *yoga* and for related terminology, etc., he had to knock at the doors of Nāthapanthīs? For confirmation of this fact the following lines are notable —

---

13. *bandhiyā mūla dekhiyā asthūla* ı
gagana garajanta dhuni dhyāna lāgā ıı

. . . .

gyāna soṅ gyāna mili dhyāna soṅ dhyāna mili ı
jāpa ajapā japai soī daṁbha lāī lakhai ıı
cita soṅ citta mili cittan cetana bhayā ı
ummunī dṛṣṭi soṅ bhāva dekhai ıı

— *Ibid.*, 3.6 and 5.15

14. *sahajaiṅ sahajaiṅ saba guna jāīlā* ı *bhagavanta bhagatā eka thira thāilā* ıı
— *Ibid.*, 8.4

jahaṁ nāda bindu kā hāthī ı *satagura le cala sāthī* ıı
suratinagara kā kara sayala ı *jāmeṁ ātmā kā mahala* ıı
joti akhaṇḍī jhilamilī ı *binu bātī kā parakāsa* ıı
motī kī jhālara lagī ı *tahāṁ ja darśana pāve dāsa* ıı[15]

Basis and Nature of Adoration

Kabīra basically adored the formless Rāma. In philosophical language we can consider this belief nearly as monism fostered by the monotheistic ideology.[16] But when we think deeply on the basic character of monotheism and monism then we find that it is very difficult to bring both into harmony. As such we have to again come to the conclusion of Paṇḍit Paraśurāma Caturvedī — in reality Kabīra is neither *nirguṇavādī* nor *saguṇavādī*. His Ultimate Being is far from *nirguṇa* and *saguṇa* and inexpressible in words.[17]

In this context he did not create any controversy and said directly — *vo hai jaisā vo hī jāne* ı *jasa tūṁ tasa tohiṅ koī na jāna* ı *loga kahaiṅ saba ānahin āna* ıı[18] — meaning only God knows His own character, none else knows. In absence of complete knowledge whatever appears in one's mind, he says the very same. He is not like the One as He is claimed to be by the people who boast to have perceived him. Hence, it is wise to remain quiet on this aspect.[19] It is also true that He has uncountable names. We cannot utter all of them. Association of form with name will appear only when there exists any form. A formless can be only nameless — *avigati kī gati kyā kahūṅ, jiskā gāṅva na nāṅva* ı *gunabihūna kā pekhie kākara dhariye*

---

15. *Rāmānanda Kī Hindī Racanāyen*, 8.2, 9.9, 10.21 and 10.23.
16. Pītāmbar Dutt Baḍathvāl, *Hindī Kāvya Mein Nirguṇa Sampradāya*, pp. 93-100
17. *Kabīra Sāhitya Kī Parakha*, p. 92.
18. *Kabīra Granthāvalī*, p. 241.6 and 103.47
19. *jasa kahiye tasa hota nahiṅ, jasa hai taisā soi* — *Ibid.*, 230.3

nāṅva ॥[20] His following instruction is therefore more useful for the common people :

hari jaisā hai taisā rahai । *to harași harași guna gāya* ॥[21]

20. *Kabīra Granthāvalī*, 238.5
21. *Ibid.*, 17.2.

7

Vaiṣṇava Adoration

Acharya Ganga Sharana Shastri

It is notable that in the Vaiṣṇava society there is no single adoration system, because this society is split into many factions which are on the increase. Vaiṣṇavas have neither a single *mantra* nor a single deity. Ācārī Vaiṣṇavas connect themselves with Ācārya Śaṭhakopa and extend this link up to Nārāyaṇa Vīṣṇu. They consider Sanaka etc. to be their first *ācārya*. The god of Ācārīs is Lakṣmīnārāyaṇa Viṣṇu and their *mantra* consists of twelve letters *oṁ namo nārayaṇa vāsudevāya* and their original text is *Nārāyaṇatāpanīyopaniṣad*, although Ācārya Śaṭhakopa has composed many scriptures. The famous four Vedas in Tamil are among these scriptures, but the *ācārya*s of north India do not consider Tamil Vedas as significant as *Nārāyaṇa-tāpanīyopaniṣad* and connect themselves with the Vedas holding at the same time that they are Vaidika as Nārāyaṇa Viṣṇu is referred to in ihe Vedas. The followers of other sects, on the other hand, do not admit this claim as they say that Ācārī Vaiṣṇavas had come into existence very late.

Similarly, there had been one Nimbārka Svāmī among Vaiṣṇavas. He has his own *mantra* and his deity is Bhagavān Kr̥ṣṇa. His main scripture is *Śrīmad Bhāgavata Mahāpuraṇa*. He also believed in *Rādhātāpanīyopaniṣad, Kr̥ṣṇatāpanīyopaniṣad, Brahmavaivarta Purāṇa, Garga Saṁhitā*, etc. His *mantra* also belongs to Rādhā-Kr̥ṣna and he also assumed himself Vaidika. His doctrine is similar to Ācāryajī's doctrine. Similarly,

Vallabha Svāmī is also a member of Vaiṣṇavas. He has also his own *mantra* but his deity is Gopāla Jī. His scriptures are *Gopālatāpanīyopaniṣad* and *Śrīmadbhāgavata Purāṇa*. Whichever scriptures the other Vaiṣṇavas believed, he also approved them. In the same way, Mādhavācārya's sect is also in existence among Vaiṣṇavas. Śrī Viṣṇu Svāmī Jī also has a different adoration system. He also believed in those scriptures which have been adopted by the other Vaiṣṇavas. Mādhavācārya's scripture is *Sarvadarśana-sāra-saṁgraha*, which is excellent from the viewpoint of collection and almost all the Vaiṣṇavas read it.

Among the *ācāryās*, Rāghavācārya is the *guru* of Svāmī Rāmānandācārya, who has an important place among the Vaiṣṇavas. His principles have been developed and diffused by Svāmī Rāmānandācārya. Swāmī Rāmānanda has been considered seniormost among all the Vaiṣṇavas. His area of activities seems to cover all over India. He has composed several significant scriptures. His original texts are the *Rāma-tāpanīyopaniṣad*, *Adhyātma Rāmāyaṇa*, *Vaiṣṇava Matābja-Bhāskara* and the *Rāmapaṭala* which is related to conduct. Svāmī Rāmānanda has also written commentary on several scriptures, among which *Śrībhāṣya* is significant. Several erudite scholars connect themselves with the Vedas. Taking support of the *Prauḍhavāda* (maturism), in the Vedas, they accomplish Rāma, Sītā, Daśaratha, etc.; nowhere in the Vedas it has been so referred to. Some of their *ācārya*s have also made commentary on the Vedas, in which accomplishment of Rāma-Sītā has been done.

We mean to say that all Vaiṣṇavas connect themselves in some way or the other with the Vedas because the Vedas have been considered as the best and most authentic scriptures of the Indian literature. Vaiṣṇavas have contributed significantly to the prosperity of the Hindu society. They tried to remove the vices of untouchability and casteism. Rāmānandācārya tried to bring together those castes and *varṇa*s (four classes into which the Indo-Āryan society was divided) which were divided into faction by the Vedic brāhmaṇas. But Gosvāmī Tulasīdāsa ravaged all the efforts of Svāmī Rāmānandācārya. He re-established the four *varṇa*s and declared some castes inferior by name. This caused Rāmānandī Vaiṣṇavas to reach again to the old system. At present among the Rāmānandīs only the brāhmaṇas can enter into the kitchen. They initiate the people of other castes so as to get the labour work of *āśrama* done by them. It can be thus said that the Rāmānandī Vaiṣṇava has gone to worse. They have limited themselves to the *Rāmāyaṇa* of Tulasīdāsa and they recognize the same as their original text. Rāmānandācārya's ideal is found nowhere and the doctrines of the four Vaiṣṇava sects are one or the other, qualified non-dualism, double dualism, pure monism, double monism peculiarity, etc.

Similarly, they have four types of salvation — *sālokya, sāmīpya, sāyujya* and *sārūpya*. There are also many other facts which are difficult to grasp. Commentary of Uttaramīmāṁsā composed by Rāmānujācārya and commentaries on other scriptures could be seen as examples. Mahāprabhu Caitanyadeva had also been in north India. His deity is Bhagavān Kṛṣṇa and the source text is mainly *Śrīmad Bhāgavata*. He stressed on singing devotional songs (*saṁkīrtana*). In the present age his songs have spread all over the world except the Muslim countries. His ideology based on humanism, is praiseworthy. Recenctly, a saint, named Prabhupāda has promoted the Vaiṣṇava *dharma* a lot. He propounded against casteism and untouchability and diffused the sect of Caitanya Mahāprabhu in America and Europe. Large number of foreigners are his disciples and are working well even today. Similarly, in the south-west India there are some important branches of Vaiṣṇavas. Bārkarī sect is one of them in which there have been famous propagators like Sant Jñāneśvara, Nāmadeva, Tukārāma, Jokhāmelā, Gaurā Kumhāra, Rāmadāsa to name a few. They have defended the Indian religion from heresy. There have been several important branches of Vaiṣṇavas even in Tamil Nadu, Andhra, Kerala, Orissa, etc. As, for example, saints like Pañcaśikhācārya was very famous in Orissa.

In Tamil Nadu also apart from Ācārya Śaṭhakopa several other saints have also been in the Vaiṣṇava sect. Rāma, Kṛṣṇa, Sītā, and Rādhā were worshipped by all of them. There are some more sects among the Vaiṣṇavas like Narasī Mehtā, Jūnāgarh Gujarat, Kabīrapanthī, Dādupanthī, Ravidāsapanthī, Rāmsnehīpanthī, Nānakapanthī, Śivanārāyaṇapanthī, Garībdāsapanthī, Jagjīvandāsapanthī. They worshipped the formless *Brahman*. He is omnipresent, omniscient, omnicompetent, omnipotent and beyond the *avatāras*. Neither does he take birth nor dies. The same *Brahman* has been adored by the people of the aforesaid sects. They have also many *mantras* and they believed in the preachings of their own *ācāryas*. They considered Nirguṇapanthī Vaiṣṇava's Veda as inferior. They give preference to the speeches of their *guru* and follow the opinions of saints. They do not believe in casteism and untouchability, and named their deity according to their adoration. Among them some people stressed the word *guru* very much and repeatedly uttered *guru guru*. Their *mantra* is also almost non-Vedic because they considered the Vedas as mere ritual practices (*karma-kāṇḍa*) and hence neglected them. Since some of them utter *oṁ* in the beginning of their *mantra*, hence, they cannot be considered non-Vedic.

In my opinion the whole Vaiṣṇava society is within the circle of *nirguṇa-saguṇa* and they have their individual adoration system. Although, after Svāmī Rāmānandācārya the image-worship has been preferred by the Vaiṣṇavas, which is literally against the Vedic *dharma* as such is not mentioned in the Vedas and even there is no reference to the *avatāras*, yet at present the Vaiṣṇava society is fully immersed in the *avatāravāda* and image-worship. For this reason the Indian adoration of Ultimate Being has ended and worship of the images of *devadūtas* (angels) has come into vogue which is also totally against the Vedas which advocate the adoration of formless *Brahman*. It is sad that at present it is not even a matter of discussion among the Vaiṣṇavas. Today the whole Hindu society is attached to image-worship. Even the worshippers of *nirguṇa Brahman* have also limited their worship to images and pictures. They have even gone to the extent of believing in *samādhis* abandoning their adoration of *nirguṇa Brahman*. This has resulted in the weakening of the Hindu society. Hindu society is not getting proper education of *dharma*. At present only that education is being given which helps in earning money.

We do hope that the time has come when the Hindu society should recognize its ancient tradition. Only then the welfare of every human being is possible. At present the Hindu's moral has fallen to such an extent that the followers of other *dharmas* look down upon them. Hindus are decaying morally for the last twelve centuries. We should improve ourselves and only after proper intellectual inspection should begin with the adoration. We had once diffused our *dharma* over Asia and European countries, but at present we have shrunk a lot and are still shrinking unceasingly. It is now enough, we should awake to adopt that significant adoration system which we had spread even up to Europe.

At first the basic worship of Vaiṣṇavas had been mental and there had also been mentally muttered prayer. But gradually the mental worship deviated from its original form and came to be based on *Haṭha-yoga*. Practices like *neti, dhauti-nevali,* etc., became significant. Later it further changed to image-worship and at present has gone to such an extent that God has been even connected with the human feelings. God started to conduct like man. God is now made to wash His hands and feet, clean the teeth, take bath; afterwards *bālabhoga* and refreshment is offered to Him; around 12 noon full meal is offered to Him and then he is made to sleep; God again is awakened at 4 p.m. and is offered refreshment; in the evening also He is offered food. To fan with a handfan in the summer night or to set the cooler on; to clothe in warm clothes in the winter season or to cover with woolen sheet and quilt; and the offering of food by one to God first then to Himself are the common practices nowadays. Thus, presenting the Ultimate Being in the form of man has become the basic *dharma* of Vaiṣṇavas, although Svāmī Rāmānanda Jī and all the *ācārya*s of Vaiṣṇavas have emphasized on the mental muttered prayer. Even today the Kabīra Vaiṣṇavas prefer *ajapājapa suratiyoga*. I think all this has been guided by Svāmī Rāmānanda otherwise how could Kabīra have adopted it, because he himself has confessed that he attained knowledge through his *guru*. Principles of original Vaiṣṇavas are in existence in Kabīrapantha even today. Vaiṣṇavas expounded monotheism. Vaiṣṇavas said :

> *vidhi hari śaṁbhu nacāvana hāre* ।
> *jaga pekhani tuma pekhani hāre* ॥
> *hari vyāpaka sarvatra samānā* ।
> *prema te pragata hoya hama jānā* ॥

This proclamation was made by the Vaiṣṇava society. But later on some Vaiṣṇavas made strange imagination which is a matter of understanding like the imagination of *arcāvatāra*, *gadāvatāra*, *cakrāvatāra*, etc. For such reasons I say that the Vaiṣṇavas also adopted polytheism. There is one more notable fact that God Viṣṇu who has been mentioned as formless and partless (*nirākāra* and *nirālamba*) in the Vedas has been in the Purāṇas torn to shreds. There is a *mantra* in the *Yajurveda* which reveals that the whole universe is diffused within a single part of Viṣṇu and the remaining three parts are hidden as it could not be perceived by anyone. The same Viṣṇu is diffused in all directions and sub-directions and is present in the hearts of all creatures. The composers of Purāṇas delineated Viṣṇu as woman, child, baby, etc., and the subsequent Vaiṣṇavas also followed it. For the same reason the adoration system of Vaiṣṇavas abandoned monotheism and evolved various forms of worship thereby making the recognition difficult as to which Vaiṣṇavas adore whom. Particularly, the Vaiṣṇava sects in Kāśī behave according to the aforesaid statement. As such it has never been possible to uniform the Vaiṣṇava's adoration.

8

Kāśī: The Abode of Līlās

Bhanu Shankara Mehta

In one of its decisions Allahabad High Court has observed that *līlā* is a procession which is organized in all cities of India. At the same time the court also remarked that it is not an image worship in a temple. On the other hand, there is the dramatic world which liberally assumed *līlā* as folk drama but it also says that it is an "immature drama." It is notable that while hardly hundreds of people assemble in a theatre hall, a crowd of thousands of people assemble to see the *Rāmalīlā* or *Rāsalīlā*. If we take into account the entire world, we shall find that in ancient times *līlā*s of the adored deities were played, for acquiring wealth, prosperity, attaining knowledge and salvation, in many countries like Egypt, Sumera, Accadia, Greece, Philistine, Haiti, and many other countries of Europe.

Indian Purāṇas are filled with the mentions of *Devalīlā*s. *Śivalīlā*s have been played since ancient times in Tamil Nadu. In Maharashtra, *Lalita* or *Daśāvatāralīlā*s are played even today. Of the *Daśāvatāra* (ten *avatāras*) *līlā*s, the *līlā*s of Rāma and Kṛṣṇa are very famous. Well, as will be discussed later besides the *līlā*s of Kṛṣṇa and Rāma, the *līlā*s of Nṛsiṁha and Vāmana are also played in Kāśī even these days. More importantly the *līlā*s are neither dramas nor folk dramas. These are based on the narrations of *avatāra*s only. *Līlā*s of Gaṇeśa (Gaṇeśa festival), *Devī* (Durgā Pūjā), Sūrya and Śiva (Śiva Bārāta) is played with special meaning. Above all, *Rāmalīlā* and *Rāsalīlā* are played all over the country and in foreign countries too (*līlā*s are played everywhere but the Sūtradhāra Svāmī is never perceived).

First of all we must know what actually is the *līlā* ? According to *Halāyudha Kośa*, "In the state of separation the imitation of clothing and adornments, movement, glance, laugh, dialogue, etc., of the lover for amusement is called *līlā*." According to the other lexicons, *līlā* means pleasure, amusement, bliss, recreation, behaviour, sexual intercourse, easy perception, splendour, blandishment, image beauty, loveliness, savour and illusion. It is "sport" of the God. In spiritual terms it can be said that an expresion of Supreme Spirit in different forms and His love by the inconceivable and delightful *māyāyoga* is *līlā*. According to the *Līlā Tattva Vimarśa* — *lī* means to attach with heart and *lā* means to receive. The way by which one can attain God is *līlā*. There are three kinds of *līlā* — (1) *nitya* (constant) *līlā*, i.e., *līlā* played constantly by God, which is exhibited in the day-to-day working of the world, (2) *avatarita līlā*, i.e., actions taken by the *avatāra*s of God and its related events so as to remove the deterioration of the world, (3) *anukaraṇātmaka* (imitation) *līlā*, i.e., is the immature attempt of a devotee, enthusiastic to meet God, to imitate the *līlā*s of the *avatāra* of God. These are Rāma-Kr̥ṣṇa *līlā*s in these days. *Nitya līlā* is imperishable, *avātāra līlā* is real and *anukaraṇa līlā* is practical.

What is the motive of *līlā* ? It is said :

atha līlānukaraṇaṁ pravakṣyāmi mahāmune ।
yat kr̥tvā cātha dr̥ṣtvā hi mucyate pātakairnaraḥ ॥

Basically, *līlā* is Vaiṣṇava. According to the *Pāñcarātra Saṁhitā*, there are five methods of worship of Viṣṇu — dancing, singing, playing musical instruments, procession of idols, and setting up tableaux of *pañcāyatana*. *Śrīmad Bhāgavata* (10.70.39) mentions about the motive of līlā —

jīvasya yaḥ saṁsarato vimokṣaṇa ।
na jānato'narthavahā ccharīrataḥ ॥

līlāvatāraiḥ svayaśaḥ pradīpakaṁ ।
prājvālayattvāṁ tamahaṁ prapadye ॥
— *Bhāgavata*, 10.70.39

It is mentioned — *lokavattu līlā kaivalyam* — meaning, this world is his sensuous pleasure. Infinite Vaiṣṇava literature is available on the commentary of *līlā*, those curious should study it and enjoy.

As mentioned earlier, the tradition of *līlā* is very old. Beginning of narration of Hari (*hari-kathā*) could be assumed with the singing of *Rāmāyaṇa* by Lava-Kuśa. Iṅ the *Harivaṁśa Purāṇa* the meeting between Kauvera and Rambhā has been described in detail. In the Purāṇa, composed by Vyāsa, there are descriptions of different *līlā*s, like *Śivalīlā* in the *Liṅga Purāṇa*; *Devīlīlā*s in *Devī Purāṇa*, *Kālikā Purāṇa* and *Devī Bhāgavata*; *Gaṇeśalīlā* in *Gaṇeśa Purāṇa*; and *Viṣṇulīlā* in *Viṣṇu Purāṇa*. Narrations of *avatāra*s is often staged in the folk dramas. Narrations of *avatāra*s and gods can be seen in the classical and doctrinal dramas too.

Naṭyaśāstra mentions *rāsa* or *rāsaka* and the dances *tāṇḍava* and *lāsya*. The same *lāsya* has been named as *garbā* dance and the *maṇḍala rāsaka* as *hallīsaka* in Gujarat. The chapters 29 to 33 of the tenth *skandha* (section) in *Śrīmad Bhāgavata* are called as "Rāsapañcādhyāyī." These mention about the *mahārāsa* performed on the day of full moon in winter season. Certainly, *mahārāsa* is the best form of Vaiṣṇava *līlā*. Staging of *Rāsalīlā* began in the tenth century. That which is full of savour is *rāsa*. *Rāsa* is a dance and when some narration is included it becomes *Rāsalīlā*. The Vaiṣṇava saints like Jayadeva, Caitanya, Caṇḍīdāsa, Vidyāpati, Śaṅkaradeva were between twelfth and fifteenth centuries. Mahāprabhu Vallabhācārya, the founder of *Puṣṭimārga*, bestowed the poetry world with Sūradāsa and the region of Braja with *Rāsalīlā*. His son Śrī Viṭṭhalanātha developed *Rāsalīlā*. In the same tradition Meghā Bhagat (Saṁvat 1600) introduced *Rāmalīlā* in Kāśī on the basis of the great epic *Rāmāyaṇa*. Later on Gosvāmī Tulasīdāsa initiated *Rāmalīlā* to diffuse the message of *Rāmacaritamānasa*. Thus, *līlā* is being played for the last 450 years. The king of Kāśī reorganized *Rāmalīlā* with the help of Bharatendu Harishchandra, Kartajihva Svami, Raghunatha Singh of Riva, Pandit Harihar Prasad and Baba Kharabadasa in the nineteenth century, which is unique in the world.

Gosvāmī Tulasīdāsa began *Rāmalīlā* with *rājyābhiṣeka līlā* which has been found to be mentioned in the *Gautama Candrikā*. It is notable that Tulasīdāsa saved *dharma* in that dark era by composing *Rāmāyaṇa* in manuscript on one hand and by organizing *līlā* for the illiterate people so that they could understand the meaning of *dharma* on the other. He directed — *jāko artha jahaṁ hai jaiso, līlā lalita lakhāvati taiso.*

Story of *līlā* is eternal like those of Hari. So a brief introduction of the *līlā*s of Kāśī is being presented here.

Rāmalīlā

Hundreds of parties play *Rāmalīlā* from time to time, specially in the month of Āśvina every year in Kāśī. The duration of these *Rāmalīlā*s is five to thirty days. The main kinds of such *līlā*s are as under.

JHĀṄKĪ LĪLĀ

Chitrakuta Ramalila Committee has been organizing the said *līlā* for the past 450 years. It lasts 22 days. Its "Bharata Milāpa" episode is universally famous. The very same Lila Committee had seen Hanumānjī jumping over the river Varuṇā in 1811 and it also obtained a decision from Allahabad High Court in 1910. In this *līlā* the tableau of *Daśāvatāra* is staged on the last day.

TULASĪ'S CĪRA GHĀṬA LĪLĀ

This is also being enacted for the last 400 years uninterruptedly. It continues 22 days. Its Tulaśī stage is simply wonderful.

GHAṬITA LĪLĀ OF RĀMNAGAR

It is being held since the last 150 years. Its duration of enactment is 30 days. The entire Rāmnagar appears to be a stage during this *līlā*. It is famous all over the world.

Citrakūṭa's Narsiṁha, Vāmana and Phāga Līlā

Narsiṁha līlā is played on Narsiṁha platform in Naraharipurā on *Narsiṁha Caturdaśī*. Its present form is *Narsiṁha līlā*, composed by Śrī Keśava Rāi in 1917 which is recited along with *līlā*. It is notable that Gosvāmī Tulasīdāsa had lived here (Naraharipurā) for some time.

VĀMANA LĪLĀ

This *līlā* is played by the Citrakuta Lila Committee on *Vāmana Dvādaśī*. It is a *līlā* that is enacted only for a day.

PHĀGA LĪLĀ

This *līlā* is also played by the Citrakuta Committee on the occasion of *Holī*. It is based on the episode describing the *Holī* played between Sītā and Rāma. This *līlā* gets converted into a procession at the end.

Kṛṣṇalīlā of Tulasīghat

It is based on the *Braja Vilāsa* — composed by Śrī Brajavāsī Dāsa. It was initiated by Mahant Dhanīrām Jī. Its world famous *līlā* is — "Nāga Nathaiyā." It is to be noted that it is different from the traditional *Rāsalīlā* and is played on the line of *Rāmalīlā* of Kāśī. Its applause is — *bolade vṛndāvana bihārīlāla kī jaya*. This *līlā* is also staged for 21 days. Its 17th episode is related to the tableau (*jhāṅkī*) of *Daśāvatāra*. Gosvāmī Tulasīdāsa has composed *Kṛṣṇa Gītāvalī* for it which is recited in this *līlā*.

It is notable that Gosvāmī Tulasīdāsa also organized *dharma* and *Prahlāda līlā* along with *Rāmalīlā* and *Kṛṣṇalīlā* which is not in vogue now.

Narasiṁha Līlā of Prahlāda Ghat

The enthusiastic people of Prahlāda Ghat organized the delightful *Prahlādalīlā* in the twentieth century. Its duration of enactment is five days.

Rāsalīlā

Rāsa parties from Vṛndāvana and Mathura often arrive in Kāśī and present *Rāsalīlā* in the morning and *Rāmalīlā* in the evening. *Rāsalīlā* has more than hundred sections. There has been a beautiful combination of dance and singing in *Rāsalīlā* and *Rāmalīlā* presented by the *Rāsa* parties. There is a tradition of *Mānasa Pāṭha* in Nāradavānī here.

This chapter will be incomplete without mentioning the adornment in temples. In the Vaiṣṇava temples of Kāśī, during the month of Kārttika tableaux (*jhāṅkī*) of *līlā* were decorated with the help of wood. The writer himself has seen the *Gajagrāhalīlā* and *Cīraharaṇalīlā*. Unfortunately, this genre seems to have disappeared. In the temple of Ganga Mahala Ghat, even today on the occasion of *Janmāṣṭamī* festival, the images are decorated such that they exhibit different forms. It is the image of Viṣṇu that is often shown as riding, sitting and lying on his Garuḍa. In the tradition of Gopāla temple, in the daily service, every time a new episode is decorated all anew (in the tradition of Śrīnātha Jī). The devotees immensely enjoy watching such adornments. It is true that during *līlā* man enjoys great savour and the divine form is also perceived often. If you have good fortune only then you can sing with Kabīra :

dulahinagāvahu mangalacāra,
hama ghara āye rājārāma bhatāra ।

I would like to conclude this chapter with the *pada* of Bharatendu Harishchandra :

hari līlā saba vidhi sukhadāī ।
kahata sunata dekhata jiya ānata
deti bhagati adhikāi ॥
prema baḍhata agha nasata, punya rati
jiya men upajata āī ।
yāhī so haricanda karata suni nita haricarita baḍāī ॥

— *Rāmalīlā*, No. 1936

9

Puṣṭimārgīya Vaiṣṇava Tradition in Kāśī

Brajratnadasa Gupta

MAHĀPRABHU Vallabhācārya was the fourth in the series of *ācaryas*. Most of the *ācāryas* came from the south and made north their area of action. In the same chain Mahāprabhu Vallabhācārya also came to light. His parents had to flee from Kāśī due to violence of Yavanas. On the way, after a period of eight months, he was born near Champaran (near Raipur in M.P.). At the time of birth, there was no response of Life in his body. So his parents left him under a tree and resumed their journey. They received a spiritual message on their way that the baby whom they have left behind is alive. As such they returned and till then they had received yet another message that the violence made by the Yavanas has reduced in Kāśī. So they came back to Kāśī along with their son. Thus had the life of Mahāprabhu Vallabhācārya started in Kāśī. There are two *baiṭhakas* (seats) in Kāśī. One of them is at Jatanavar where the *upanayana saṁskāra* of Mahāprabhu Vallabhācārya was performed. The second is at Panchaganga Ghat, where he was married.

Although saints had come from south, their activities began from here. Especially, Mahāprabhu Vallabhācārya was initiated here and later founded his doctrine also, which is known as Purified Monism. Ācārya Śaṅkara had restrained the current of Buddhist philosophy and re-established Vedic *dharma*. According to his path only *Brahman* is the truth and rest of all is false. In course of time this belief came into vogue. On his belief he established four *maṭha*s in the four corners of the country and visited all over the country several times. During his visits he re-established the Hindu culture. Such belief empowered the Hindu culture once again. But in the later times some how people started to believe that if anyone wanted to attain salvation he had to first renounce the world. It was because of this belief that the householder group of our society, which is assumed as the foundation of the society, felt weariness and indifference. Certainly, it weakened the society. That was the age of Yavanas (Muslims) and the whole art, culture, and views of our scholars were influenced by the emperor of Delhi. The entire current of views, which ought to have flowed towards God, was flowing to that side (Delhi).

In such a period Mahāprabhu Vallabhācārya presented a new doctrine to foster the household life, which was named Purified Monism by him, in which it is mainly believed that there is *Brahman* and there is soul (*jīva*). The soul blooms because of that *Brahman*. Soul is originated from the *Brahman* and all that is happening in this world, is in fact the interaction between the soul and *Brahman*. Thus, soul is originated from *Brahman* and this world is its sphere of action, the central place of its *līlā*. So this world cannot be untrue. The soul, world as well as *Brahman* are true. So he advocated Purified Monism and established the *brahmavāda*. He named it as path of fostering (*puṣṭimārga*) on practical ground. While the other sects believed that every person has to do some work to get something from God, the Puṣṭi sect assumed the grace of God to be bestowed above all. He said that we must only aim at seeking the mercy of God for the gaining of which there is no need of making any accomplishment. If our attention is directed towards Him then we would get His blessings if He so desires. Thus, the

Puṣṭi sect established an astonishing fact in which adoration and the adored became one. When the people were preoccupied with the desire of salvation he established the Puṣṭi sect in which there is no imagining of salvation; rather it has only one aim — that of gaining the grace of God. He expounded in brief the method of availing this compassion. He included service (*sevā*), association with good people (*satsaṅga*) and remembering (*smaraṇa*) in this method.

It is said that when Mahāprabhu Vallabhācārya was visiting Vrindavan a thought arose in his mind that this soul is wicked by nature. But why it is so? This is wicked because instead of aspiring to God it is opposed to Him due to the passion of organs. He was keen to know as to how he could remove the wickedness of the soul. As the narration goes that Mahāprabhu Vallabhācārya had met here Śrīnāth Jī who motivated him to present the soul before him and also connect the soul with him. He prescribed the name *Brahmasambandha* for this connection. Śrīnāth Jī explained that when this soul would join with him the whole wickedness would be abolished and there would remain no difference between that soul and him. He also explained a method to join with *Brahman*. He asked to give the soul the *mantra* of *Brahmasambandha*. It is only thereafter, that the soul will make a self-request and the moment it makes so, the whole of its existence will immerse in the Ultimate *Brahman*. Thus will the soul gain grace of Ultimate *Brahman*.

Later, Mahāprabhu Vallabhācārya expanded this concept. Some people believe that Sūradāsa was initiated by Mahāprabhu Vallabhācārya while others believe that he was already bestowed with the intelligence of devotion, although there is reference related to this context. It is said that once he met Sūradāsa on his way. He saw that a poor brāhmaṇa was cursing himself. He recognized the marvellous brilliance of poetry hidden in him and cautioned him that first of all he was blind and secondly he was cursing himself, but the body received from God was not made for cursing. He should use his brilliance for composing *pada*s in praise of God. It is said that Mahāprabhu Vallabhācārya narrated the whole story of the *Śrīmadbhāgavata* to Sūradāsa. It is also said that Sūradāsa composed lakhs of *pada*s. I am not sure, but I have learnt somewhere that about 3500 *pada*s has been collected, refined and got printed by Sitaram Chaturvedi. But no definite number of *pada*s has been ascertained. What can be said with certainty is that he had composed uncounted *pada*s. As he was *sūra*, a blind person, a thought arose about him in my mind and I asked him :

jo sūra loga kahate hain tumheṅ kyoṅ śūra?
kyā yaha thā tumhārā sañcita puruṣārtha
yā kyā yaha thā tumhārā apanā puruṣārtha
yā pūrvajanma kā sañcita paramārtha
maine sunā tumheṅ eka vallabha milā thā,
vaha tumheṅ gigiyāte dekha karuṇā se hilā thā,
vaha tumhārī jarjara kāyā se dravita huā thā,
usane tumheṅ divya dr̥ṣṭi dāna kara,
sūra se śūra banāne kā niścaya kiyā thā
usane tumheṅ vaha jo divya dr̥ṣṭi dāna diyā
aura vaha sūrasāgara bana tumhāre kaṇṭha se phūṭa nikalā
usameṅ hilorita ho rahā thā mādhurya kr̥ṣṇa līlā kā
māno baha rahā ho śarkarāyukta navanīta pighalā ।

What I mean to say is that it was a beginning. The task which Mahāprabhu Vallabhācārya wanted to perform was further expanded through the *Sūrasāgara* of Sūradāsa symbolically. After that he inspired many poets. The *aṣṭachāpa* poets had been in Kāśī. I do not know the ancient history, except that after his birth he visited all over India twice or thrice but how he established Purified Monism and when he participated in *śāstrārtha* (doctrinal debate), or how his Purified Monism made progress, is not exactly known. Although, there is a reference to one Gopāla temple said to have been established about 175 years ago. After the establishment of Gopāla temple in Kāśī it was developed as a working place of the Puṣṭi and Vaiṣṇava sects. Around the Gopāla temple itself most of the Gujarati, Marwari, Agrawal families dwelled. Gopāla temple was the main centre of this Puṣṭi sect and from here it was diffused.

It has two aspects. The first aspect belongs to service. The notion of fostering (*puṣṭi*) service was spread among the Vaiṣṇavas firmly through Gopāla temple and it was fostered through the *aṣṭayāma* service progammes of Gopāla temple that were held on the occasions of Dīpāvalī, Graharāja worship and other festivals, be it the occasion of staging different tableaux (*jhāṅkī*s) or just swinging in the month of Śrāvaṇa. Thus through different programmes and through the programme of *darśana,* started from early in the morning and continuing up to late night, attempts were made to inspire the middle-class society dwelling around the Gopāla temple with the notion of *puṣṭi* (fostering). Not only this, I would like to explain yet another aspect of this service. Motivated by Mahāprabhu Vallabhācārya these families established the image of Gopāla Kṛṣna in their homes. They performed the *aṣṭayāma sevā*, like those performed in the Gopāla temple, in their homes. They even celebrated the different festivals that were held in the Gopāla temple according to their capacity. This tradition is still in vogue. Particularly, we can see *annakūṭa* (pile of grain) in several homes in the days of *annakūṭa* (a festival celebrated on the day following Dīvālī in which the foodstuffs are placed in a heap in front of an idol of Viṣṇu-Kṛṣṇa). This was one aspect. After a long, the notion of service was fostered much in service, *satsaṅga* and *smaraṇa* (remembering). In *satsaṅga* it was accepted a little, but in *smaraṇa* it was much limited because Mahāprabhu Vallabhācārya gave the *mantra* — *śrī kṛṣṇaḥ śaraṇaṁ mama* — which is known to all of us.

Most of the people thought that it was a secret *mantra*. People used to mutter this *mantra* in solitude with a garland (*mālā*) in their hand. But there came a strange change in it. Krishnapriya Beti Ji Maharaja, daughter of Maharaja Murali Manohar Ji of the aforementioned Gopāla temple, had formed a Śuddhadvaita Japa Yajña Society about 49 years ago to promote the work of Mahāprabhu Vallabhācārya. It has been mentioned in *Gītā* that *Śuddhādvaita yajña* is best of all sacrifices. Krishnapriya Beti ji Maharaja had some aims. She wanted to extend the limits of Vallabha society, because it was limited to religious activities in those days. She wanted that this society should be involved in the social, cultural, artistic and spiritual directions too but the basis of fostering should be the philosophy of Purified Monism established by Mahāprabhu Vallabhācārya. She made the first announcement that after a period of four months Śuddhādvaita Japa Yajña Society would be established and hence *aṣṭākṣara mantra* should be uttered in every home. She aimed at the utterance of four crore *mantra*s in four months. After four months a calculation was done and it was found that 32 crore *mantra*s had been uttered during that period and thus on the foundation of 32 crore *mantra*s she founded the Śuddhādvaita Japa Yajña Society.

After founding this society she extended the notion of service on ideological level. She promoted *satsaṅga*. In *satsaṅga* she brought another remarkable change. Until that time only the *ācārya*s of Vallabha sects were invited in *satsaṅga* but when Krishnapriya Beti Ji Maharaja founded the Śuddhādvaita Japa Yajña Society, she invited the *ācārya*s of other sects too. She tried that the Vaiṣṇavas would get a radiance of Vedic literature through these efforts that may extend their thinking. I am happy to say that in this sequence even after her absence some programmes are still being organized by Sharada Vallabha Beti Ji. Even people like Śaṅkarācārya made this stage splendid. I have heard other pious persons along with Nirañjana Deva Tīrtha, at the same place. Before it, there was a doubt that Vallabha and Śaṅkara sects cannot be coordinated. But the doubt got removed with these efforts. There was a matter of dignity which I would like to clear at this place. What a difficult situation it was? There were differences with regard to sitting order, as which sect ought to be regarded senior among them. If the followers of both, Vallabha and Śaṅkarācārya Jī, are present in the same enclave then where would be the sitting place for Śaṅkarācārya. Should it be equivalent, upper or lower? Most of them believed that the followers of Vallabha were superior to those of their counterpart and as such the latter should be alloted some lower place. But ignoring such tradition Beti Ji Maharaja honoured them with upper place and tried to foster our Hindu culture in all possible aspects.

She brought another change too. She converted the secret *mantra* — *śrī kṛṣṇaḥ śaraṇaṁ mama* — into a form of *kīrtana* to be sung by all aloud. She presented it like the *mantra* for *saṁkīrtana*. Through *satsaṅga* constant *saṁkīrtana*s were performed uninterrupted by the groups of people assembled for this purpose, for an hour or more or even for 24 hours. This even created some dispute. Several Gosvami Maharajas condemned this practice. But she did not deviate from her way. Then the second aspect came forward. Her efforts abolished the deficiency related to remembering (*smaraṇa*).

Thus, she encouraged *smaraṇa* along with service. Just opposite to the Gopāla temple, Krishnapriya Ji and Sharada Vallabha Beti Ji Maharaja constructed the Gita Bhawan where various programmes were organized in which all the three aspects — *sevā* (service), *satsaṅga* and *smaraṇa* were co-ordinated. Furthermore, they made efforts for women's education too. They felt that the illiteracy of women was the main cause for decay in society. So they emphasized woman literacy. They founded Vallabha Vidyapitha and involved people of all age groups — children, elders, old men-women, in their programmes. They even organized separate programmes for them and urged them for social work. Thus, the Puṣṭi sect which has been discussed here was founded by Mahāprabhu Vallabhācārya. The current of this sect is still flowing through the Puṣṭi Vaiṣṇavas in Kāśī and it has made distinctive contribution in the tradition of Kāśī and to the radiance of Kāśī.

10

Contribution of Vaiṣṇava Saints of Maharashtra to Kāśī

Nilakanth Purushottam Joshi

THERE is a famous branch of Vaiṣṇavas of Maharashtra namely Vārakarī sect. The history of this sect is about 800 years old, the main area of this sect is Paṇḍharapura and the adored deity being Viṭṭhala who is Śrī Kṛṣṇa Himself and who reached Paṇḍharapura to show grace to Bhakta Puṇḍalīka. Puṇḍalīka was serving his parents at that time. As such he indicated a brick to Śrī Kṛṣṇa lying nearby and asked him to wait, standing on the brick. Standing there and laying his hand at waist the god waited for his *bhakta*. This is the form of Viṭṭhala. Having conch-shell and lotus in both his hands and laying hand on waist the deity is waiting for his *bhakta*. This deity is known as Pāṇḍuraṅga or Viṭṭhala, Viṭhobā or Viṭhū, etc. On Devaśayaṇī Ekādaśī and Devotthānī Ekādaśī of Āṣādha and Kārttika months respectively, devotees come to Paṇḍharapura on foot, wearing the garland of basil plant and having flags in their hands. This pilgrimage is named as "Vārī" and the pilgrims as "Vārakarī." There is no distinction of *varṇa* (caste) in Vārakarī sect. Considering each man as God, devotees touch the feet of each other. This sect had continuous connection with Kāśī too. There are at least three temples and seven adored images of Bhagavān Viṭṭhala here even today, among which Viṭṭhala temple of Durga Ghat is the most famous.

Among the images adored even today, those at Durga Ghat, Dudhavinayaka, Bibihatiya, Panchaganga Ghat, Saṅkaṭā temple, Dashavamedha Ghat deserve mention.

In the thirteenth century saints of Vārakarī sect were very much influential in Maharashtra. Men and women of different castes like brāhmaṇa, *darẓī* (tailor), *kumhāra* (potter), *mālī* (gardener), *mahāra, baniyā* were prominently included among them. Bahiṇābāī, disciple of Samartha Rāmadāsa, with the help of rehetoric metaphor, in her *abhaṅga*, has compared the Vārakarī sect with the Deva Bhavana (place of God) — with Jñāneśvara as its foundation, Nāmadeva as expansions, Ekanātha as pillars and Tukārāma as its top. Apart from these devotees of Viṭṭhala some devotees of Rāma had also established close connections with Kāśī.

I am beginning from Jñāneśvara. His elder brother was Nivṛttinātha who was his *guru* too. Sopānadeva was his younger brother and Muktā younger sister. Father of Jñāneśvara or Jñānadeva, Viṭṭhalapanta was alienated from the world even before his marriage. The name of his wife was Rukmiṇī. No child was born to him and detachment grew within Viṭṭhalapanta. He left Ālandī silently and reached Kāśī for initiation. He was initiated by Śrīpādasvāmī and named as Caitanyāśrama. On the other side several efforts were made in search of Viṭṭhalapanta. Here Śrīpādāsvāmī did not know that Caitanya has a wife and has renounced the world without prior permission of his wife. By chance Śrīpādasvāmī came to know this fact when he went to Rāmeśvara for pilgrimage. He returned to Kāśī and ordered Caitanyāśrama to abandon his robe of ascetics and directed him to live with Rukmiṇī and he began his household life once again but faced blames, boycott and terrible dishonour in society. In such unfavourable circumstances four children were born to him in Śaka Saṁvata 1195, 1197, 1199 and 1201, i.e., in AD 1273, 1275, 1277 and 1279. Jñāneśvara was born on Janmāṣṭamī (the eighth day in dark half of the month Bhādrapada) in AD 1275 (all the dates varied two/three years). He entered the state of *samādhi* in Ālandī at the age of 21 years on the 13th day in dark half of the month Kārttika in AD 1298.

Jñāneśvara was a *yogī* of Nātha sect as well as a *saguṇa* worshipper of Viṭṭhala. He spread Viṭṭhala *bhakti* through his *abhaṅgas*. The commentary of *Bhagavad-Gītā* titled as *Bhāvārthadīpikā* or *Jñāneśvarī* (Śaka 1212 = AD 1290) composed by him in metre *Ovī* has the same place in Maharashtra which in the north was used in the *Rāmacaritamānasa* of Gosvāmī Tulasīdāsa. Jñāneśvara encouraged the saint Nāmadeva (in AD 1292) and others to come to Kāśī which will be discussed later. His residence in Kāśī is not known. Sant Nāmadeva mentioned in his *abhaṅgas* that he had visualized Viśvanātha Jī just at the entry point of Kāśī from the direction of Rāmnagara. Nāmadeva was the prominent personality in Vārakarī sect (AD 1270-1350). He was *darjī* (tailor) by caste. He had fellow feeling with Bhagavān Pāṇḍuraṅga as a friend from childhood. In the beginning he could not feel God everywhere. For this Muktā, sister of Jñāneśvara, made fun of him through Gorobā Kumhāra in the saint's society. Later, he was instructed by Bisobā Khecara (Viśvanātha Cāṭi) and his intention to realise God in every particle became firm.

The working area of Nāmadeva was very wide. He lived in Punjab for several years where he became very famous. As a result some of his *abhaṅgas* have been collected in *Guru Grantha Sāhib*. He also composed several poems in Hindi. Apart from the brothers Jñāneśvara, etc., contemporary to Nāmadeva in Maharashtra were Gorobā Kumhāra of Terḍokī, Sāvatāmālī of Iraṇbheṇḍī, Jogā Parmanānanda of Bārśī, Cokhāmelā Mahāra couple of Mangalabeḍhā, Parisā Bhāgavata, Gujarati Kumhāra Pākā and Narahari of Paṇḍharapura, etc. All of them were devotees of Viṭṭhala. Janābāī, the sweeper at Nāmadeva's home has also a high place among the saints. Jñāneśvara sent off saint Nāmadeva for Varanasi pilgrimage and a group of saints departed for many pilgrim places including Varanasi.

That pilgrimage is mentioned in Nāmadeva's *abhaṅga*s titled as *Tīrthāvalī* but no proof is available in Kāśī for that pilgrimage. After the death of Jñāneśvara and both of his brothers and sister Muktā (after Jñāneśvara the three died in a period of eight months) Nāmadeva departed again for pilgrimage and went to Punjab. His other visits to Kāśī are not known.

Ekanātha was a prominent personality among the saints who visited Kāśī after Nāmadeva. Saint Ekanātha lived in the Paiṭhaṇa region of Maharashtra, which is known as southern Kāśī too, during AD 1533-99. In the metaphor mentioned earlier he has been accepted as pillar of the building of Vārakarī sect. He has also been called, "Śāntibrahma" for his calm nature. Janārdanasvāmī of Daulatabada, who was the contemporary official and devotee of Bhagavān Dattātreya, was his *guru*. Śrī Kṛṣṇa was deity of Ekanātha. An erudite scholar and poet of Sanskrit, Ekanātha has composed a lot of poetic literature. He composed his *abhaṅga*s in Marathi as well as Hindi. The poem titled *bhāruḍa* has a special place in his collection of poetry. The word *bhāruḍa* means a meaningless presentation. It could be called *ulaṭabāṇī*, throwing light on the relationship of the soul to the ultimate beings of the saints. Dialogue genre has been adopted in chanting *bhāruḍa*s. These *bhāruḍa*s represented devotion and social status of those times as well as some mythological narrations, characters of some saints, *naṭa*s (actors), magicians, *faqīra*s (ascetic, especially Muslim) *jaṅgama, bhāṇḍa, laṅgaḍā*s (lames), blinds, *jogī* or *mahāra*s, and *julāhā*. Devotion and knowledge were taught through those characters. Some *bhāruḍa*s are in Hindi too, especially those which have been composed on the devotees of north India like Nānaka, Dādū Dhuniyā, Sajana Kasāī, Nāmadeva-Akbar dialogue, etc. Brāhmaṇa-Turka dialogues are bilingual. Some of those are believed to have been composed by Ekanātha but names of other saints have been mentioned at the end. The under-mentioned *bhāruḍa*, written in the name of Senā Nāī revealed a quarrel between Kabīra and Raidāsa. Kabīra was a worshipper of Rāma whereas Raidāsa of Kṛṣṇa. The opening of the *bhāruḍa* is mentioned below :

rāma bhagata kahe rāma barāī, rāma ayodhyāvāsī ।
niśidina śaṅkara dhyāna dharata haiṅ, dūjā nahiṅ avināśī ॥1 ॥
kisana bhagata kahe kisana barāī, kisana hamārā sāīṅ ।
alakha nirañjana vohī vohī, aura dūjā nahiṅ koī ॥2 ॥

Further allegations have been made :

bālakapana meṅ bāna ugāyo tāṭīkā jo mārī ।
yāga ṛṣī kā siddha kiyā rāma kī gati hai nyārī ॥
raṇḍī para jo bāna uṭhāyā bolata lāja nahīṅ āyī ।
binā bāna ke pūtanā mārī govardhana uparāī ॥

Further Dhuṇḍīrāja Gaṇeśa took the side of Raidāsa :

mūsaka caḍhe dhuṇḍī bhaiyā bolata amṛta vāṇī ।
sāca bhagata rohidāsa kahata haiṅ, kabīra bhagata na jānī ॥

satirizing the large belly of Gaṇeśa. Likewise Caṇḍī, Brahmā from the heaven of Brahmā, and Śaṅkara riding on ox came and pointed out that Raidāsa was true. At last Gopāla Jī came and revealed that both the Sants Kabīra and Raidāsa were his devotees.

Ekanātha stayed at Kāśī at least for the period of two years and eight months. The cause of his visit to Kāśī will be stated later on. It would be sufficient to mention here that he came to Kāśī in AD 1571 before the festival of *Rāmanavamī* and stayed somewhere near Maṇikarṇikā, a place of pilgrimage. It is mentioned clearly in the scripture *Rukmiṇī Svayaṁvara* composed by him :

vārānasi mahāpurī, manakarṇikecyā tīrīṁ, rāmajayaṅtī mājhārī,
graṅtha nirdhārī saṁpavīlā ॥74 ॥
te śake caupāśe-tryāṣṇava,prajāpati saṁvatasarāce nāṁva
caitramāsāce vaibhava, parva abhinava rāmanavamī ॥75 ॥

The scripture consists of 18 *prasaṅgas* (sections) and 1611 *oviyons*. The narration of the marriage of Rukmiṇī is given in it. Rukmiṇī has been mentioned as soul and Kṛṣṇa as Śiva here and marriage of the soul with Śiva is imagined in it.

Ekanāthī Bhagavān or *Nātha Bhāgvata* has been considered supreme in the scriptures of Sant Ekanātha. In fact, it is not a complete *Bhāgvata* but a commentary in 31 chapters on the eleventh Skandha of *Śrīmad Bhāgavata*. Metre employed is *Ovī* which has been the most favourite metre for most poets of Maharashtra. The initial five chapters of *Nātha Bhāgavata* had been composed in Paiṭhaṇa and remaining 26 in Kāśī. There is a hearsay that a brāhmaṇa having secured a copy of the initial five chapters of *Nātha Bhāgavata* recited them daily. He came to Kāśī along with those chapters and recited them daily on the banks of Gaṅgā and some scholars of Kāśī noted him. Translation of the scripture in *devabhāṣā* into *deśībhāṣa* (regional language) Marathi was disagreeable to them. They complained it to some renowned ascetic in the chair (*pīṭhādhipati*) in those days. He also did not like it and sent an order to the poet Ekanātha, the composer of *Pañcādhyāyī*, to come to Kāśī. He also took the scripture from that brāhmaṇa and kept that in his *maṭha*. Sant Ekanātha welcomed the order of Svāmī and departed for Kāśī assuming it the order of Viśvanātha Jī. Several persons of Paiṭhaṇa also departed with him. The number of persons joining him increased remarkably on the way. Irritated with the influence of Ekanātha Jī that Svāmī ordered to throw *Pañcādhyāyī* in Gaṅgā. Ekanātha remained undisturbed. The scripture was thrown, but it did not sink instead. Gaṅgā lifted that in her hands. All the people were overwhelmed with that incident. Ekanātha completed the remaining scripture here. We did not get any proof of this hearsay but in the last chapter of this scripture *ovīs* number 526 to 535 indicate the purport and these *ovīs* are the clear proof for completion of this scripture in Kāśī. The original *ovīs* are as under :

granthārambha pratiṣṭhānī । *tetha pañcādhyāyī sampādunī* । *uttaragranthācī karaṇī, ānandavanī vistārilī* ॥526॥ *tayā vārāṇasī muktikṣetrīm* । *maṇikarṇikā mahātīrī* । *pañcamudrāpīṭhā mājhārī* । *ekādaśāvarīṭīkā kelī* ॥534॥ *ekatām samtoṣale sajjana, svānande tuṣṭalā janārdana* । *pañcādhyāyī sampatājāṇa svamukheṅ āpaṇa varada vadalā* ॥535॥

Thus, the completion of rest of the scripture at Pañcamudrāpīṭha near Maṇikarṇikā in Kāśī is quite evident. The period for this work is also mentioned clearly —

vārāṇasī muktikṣetra । *vikrama śaka vr̥ṣa samvatsara* । *śake soḷāśe tīsottara* । *ṭīkā ekākāra janārdana kr̥pā* ॥551॥ *mahāmaṅgala kārtika māsī* । *śukla pakṣa paurṇimāsī* । *somavāra śivayogesī* । *ekādaśī samāpta kelī* ॥552॥

Naming the scripture as *Ekākāra Ṭīkā* Ekanātha mentioned that the scripture was compiled in Vikrama Saṁvatsara named Vr̥ṣa, in Saṁvata 1630 (AD 1573) on the day of full-moon in the month of Kārttika on Monday. He has also mentioned Śālivāhana Śaka 1495 in vogue in south, in the next *ovīs*. A question arises here as to which was the place Pañcamudrāpīṭha at Maṇikarṇikā? It seems possible that Siddhi Vināyaka, Ātma-vīreśvara, Cakrapuṣkariṇī, Saṅkaṭādevī and Hariścandreśvara or premises of Yamadharmeśvara had been called as Pañcamudrāpīṭha. Śrī Rameśakr̥ṣṇa Nāgara envisaged a distinctive temple of Bālātripurasundarī near Siddhi Vināyaka on the upper part of Cakrapuṣkariṇī Kuṇḍa was called as Pañcamudrāpīṭha.

Ekanātha Jī established an image of Śrī Kr̥ṣṇa on Pañcagaṅgā Ghat in Varanasi. Historicity of these facts should be investigated. He visited Kāśī again in AD 1588 to console his son, Haripaṇḍita who was living at Agnīśvara Ghat.

There had been two great saints contemporary to Chatrapati Śivājī. One of them was saint Tukārāma. He had an upper place in Vārakarī sect. He lived in Dehū village near Pune in 1608 to 1649. His *abhaṅga*s have been sung in every home of Maharashtra with great veneration. Tukārāma did not visit Kāśī but it is said that he had written a letter to Viśvanātha Jī as an *abhaṅga* on the request of pilgrims visiting Kāśī :

> *tumhī viśvanātha dīna raṅka mī anātha* ||
> *kṛpā karāla te thoḍī, pāyā paḍīlo barāḍī* ||
> *kāya ūṇeṅ tumhā pāśī, mī to alpacī santoṣī* ||
> *tukā mhaṇe devā, kāhī bhātuke pāṭhavā* ||

> You are lord of the world, I am poor beggar, I greet you. You have no shortage of anything but I am a contented person. Tukārāma requests you to send a little offering.

The second great saint, who was also a contemporary to Chatrapati Śivājī, was his Guru Samartha Rāmdāsa (AD 1608-1682). Before meeting Śivājī he (Samartha Rāmdāsa) had performed the work of general awareness and public well-being extensively wandering across India under the pretext of Āsetu Himācala pilgrimage. He built *maṭha*s at different places and established the images of Hanumān Jī. He appointed his disciples as *mahanta*s and owners of *maṭha*s at different places and thus spread out a planned network for getting and sending information. He also visited Kāśī in AD 1634 amidst his visits. He stayed here for some days. He established the image of Hanumān at Hanuman Ghat. In the list of his *mahanta*s the name of Rāmacandra of Kāśī, Rāmakṛṣṇa of Ayodhyā, Harīkṛṣṇa of Mathura and Jayakṛṣṇa of Haridvār were included. However, not much information is available about Rāmacandra of Kāśī. He himself revealed about his visit to Kāśī :

> *kelā kāśī viśveśvara, śvetabandha rāmeśvara* ||
> *bārāliṅge yā vegḷī tīrthe kelī bhūmaṇḍaḷī* ||

Nirañjana Mādhava was the Bhakta poet who made a commentary on social and historical circumstances of medieval Kāśī of eighteenth century. He was born in 1702. Nirañjana

Mādhava was an employee of Bājīrāva Peśavā of Pune and his son Nānāsāhaba Peśvā and were appointed as ambassador on behalf of Marāṭhās in the kingdom of Nizām and the British (1741-58). He was the worshipper of Datta in the beginning and was initiated in Siddheśvara sect later but he was also inclined toward Bhāgavata *dharma*. There are many literary compositions made by Nirañjana Mādhava but he is famous for his *stotras*. He came to Kāśī about AD 1740 when Gaṅgāputras and employees appointed for collection of *jaẓiyā* (tax levied on non-Muslims living under Muslim Government) troubled the people very much. Nirañjana Mādhava mentioned that situation — probably his own experience in the lines given below :

gaṅgāputra gumāna phāra karitī ghatīṅ sadā hiṇḍanī ।
kangālāsi piḍā karuni dharitī 'de dakṣiṇā' bolatī ॥
thoḍī theti na, bolatī khalamati nānāparī pīḍitī ।
āṅgāsī jhaṭatī, kicāṭa karatī, hāṇoti dheti kitī ॥
ādhī narācī gaṇatī karāvī, velī avelī rujūtī pahāvī ।
nyūnādhikeṅ kaida dutī dharārvī, tain jejayācī bharatī karāvī ॥
nikāsa be moina duḥkhakārī, dhyāvā dujā hāsila phaujadārī ।
hāsila detā curaḍā uḍāvā, koṭhūniyā dharma puḍhe karāvā ॥

The first description is the mention of the arrogant sons of Gaṅgā who used to misbehave with and ill-treat the poor people for excessive *dakṣiṇā* and also get to the extent of quarrelling and beating. Others were *hākimas* appointed for collection of *jaẓiyā*. They used to arrest the people for any fault committed in counting.

Nirañjana Mādhava called Kāśī "Kāmdhenu of people." He records that he has visited *ghats*, palaces combined with small barred windows, the old Koṭa on the banks of Gaṅgā and several inns, where different amusements arranged, seeing which the people of south India felt delighted.

Mention of the great poet Moropanta (AD 1729-94) among the saints of Maharashtra who visited Kāśī in the end of eighteenth century is necessary. Moropanta's surname was Parāḍakara. He is well-known for his savourous, although delighting but partially wretched, poems combined with rhetorics like *Śleṣa*, etc.

Apart from the complete *Mahābhārata*, he composed *Rāmakathā* in several forms which reflects his wonderful mastery of poetry. Among the several forms of *Rāmakathā Mantrarāmāyaṇa, Niroṣṭha Rāmāyaṇa, Parantu Rāmāyaṇa, Dohā Rāmāyaṇa, Savaiyā Rāmāyaṇa*, etc., deserve particular mention. The name of his wife was Ramābaī who compelled him to visit Kāśī (AD 1788). Before visiting Kāśī he had sent a letter of communique in the name of Gaṅgā Jī. After reaching Kāśī he showed his gratefulness for bestowing honour to his letter while praising Bhāgīrathī on the banks of Gaṅgā :

tuvāṁ matpatrālā janani didhalā māna kaḷale ।
tujhe kāruṇyardre mana majakaḍe spaṣṭa vaḷale ॥
sukheṅ yeṇeṅ jhāle, sakaḷahi pathīṅ vighna ṭaḷale ।
prasū prakṣāḷīla tvarita na kaśī bāḷa maḷale? ॥

Moropanta has composed the poems titled — *Gaṅgāpada Vakīlī* in Kāśī and *Viṣṇupada Vakīlī* in Gayā in which he has appealed to Gaṅgā and Viṣṇupada for the holy liberation of his *saṁbandhi* (father of daughter-in-law) Bābā Pādhye, a writer of *Dharmasindhu*, besides his parents and for bestowing devotion of Hari on his own dependents, various relatives, Ahilyābāī Hoḷkara, as well as his brother's children. He also asked death for himself on the banks of Gaṅgā in Kāśī :

tulā ālo āhe janani kara johūni śaraṇa,
svatīri tvāṁ dyāve dravuni maja kāśīta maraṇa.

The famous saint of Maharashtra Brahmacaitanya Śrī Gondavalekara Mahārāja (AD 1845-1913) visited Kāśī ten times on foot and twice by train. His *paṇḍā* in Kāśī was Paṇḍita

Masūriyādīna Śivamaṅgala. When Gondavalakara Ji came to Kāśī along with his old mother then he stayed at the temple of Nagapura's king Bhoṅsale for a month.

Thus, with Varanasi has been in close association of many saints of Maharashtra in different ways.

Bibliography

Bagholikar, H.B., *Mahārāṣtra Śāradece Mānakarī*, Part 1, Pune 1950.

Śrī Ekanāthī Bhāruḍa, Mumbai; *Śrīramadāsācī kavitā* 1, dhuḷeṅ ś. 1830.4. K.V. Belsare, Brahma Caitanya Śrī Gondavalekara Mahārāja, Saptama Punarmudraṇa, Mumbai 1983.

Vajhe, Bhaushastri, *Mājhā Citrapata va kaśīcā saṁpūrṇa itihāsa*, Pune, 1861.

11

Vaiṣṇava Havelī Music

Pradip Kumar Dikshit "Neharang"

VAIṢṆAVA Music enriched by "Aṣṭa Chāpa poets" (a group of Kṛṣṇa poets all said to be disciples of Vallabhācārya or Viṭṭhalanātha and to have lived at Govardhana in the later sixteenth century) of Vaiṣṇava sect is "Havelī Music." First of all we should understand the word "Havelī" of Phārasī. Its literal meanings are building, temple, house.

In medieval times a temple which appeared to be a *koṭhī* (bungalow) of a rich man from outside — with Lāla Jī embellished in the inner part — was deliberately so built in order to keep it safe from the attack of tyrants. The devotional (*bhakti*) music of *dhruvapada* genre is in fact the Havelī music which relates to all the activities of God and was sung here in the eight *yāma*s (period of three hours).

There are eight *darśana*s — (1) Maṅgalā (auspicious), (2) Śṛṅgāra, (3) Gvāla, (4) Rājabhoga, (5) Utthāna, (6) Bhoga, (7) Sandhyā, and (8) Śayana. In these eight sights presentation of music before God is also just an inseparable part. That tradition has been rare in vogue now and the temples of Vaiṣṇava Puṣṭi- mārga in Kāśī have also been influenced by it.

Music has always been connected with almost all the *dharma*s in India. In medieval times there were some prominent sects which made the spirit of devotion strong. Among those sects (1) Rāmānuja sect, (2) Nimbārka sect, (3) Mādhava sect, (4) Viṣṇu Svāmī sect, (5) Caitanya sect, and (6) Vallabha sect

(1479-1533) are notable. Vallabha sect has been known as Puṣṭimārga sect and the "Havelī music" of Ācārya Viṭṭhalanātha Jī and Ācārya Gokuleśa and also of *aṣṭachāpa* poets became extremely popular (playing on *pakhāvaja* before *śṛṅgāra* is not in vogue so that Ṭhākura Jī, while resting, does not feel disturbed).

Music of Puṣṭimārga can be divided in to three terms (1) preliminary (1500 to 1650), (2) medieval (1651 to 1800), and (3) later (1801 to 1950). Again preliminary period can be divided into three terms (1) first term related to Vallabhācārya (1500 to 1530); (2) second term related to Viṭṭhaleśa Jī (1531 to 1590), and (3) third term related to Gokuleśa (1591 to 1650). A brief introduction of the poets of Aṣṭachāpa has been mentioned in the table separately. Birth, feeling, castes, names, permanent residence, *guru* who initiated and the time of death of the eight poets have been collected (see the table at the end of the writeup)

According to *Khaṭ Ṛtu Vārtā*,[1] Śrī Thākura Jī had 36 *rāga*s-*rāginī*s based upon which the artists were asked to sing-play-dance six times in one season along with the 36 instruments. The 36 *rāga*s and *rāginī*s are — (1) *malhāra*, (2) *lalita*, (3) *pañcama*, (4) *āsāvarī*, (5) *bhairava*, (6) *mālava*, (7) *toḍī*, (8) *kalyāṇa*, (9) *gurjarī*, (10) *mālavī*, (11) *gauḍī*, (12) *bilāvala*, (13) *dhanāśrī*, (14) *raṅgīlī*, (15) *khammāja*, (16) *deśakāra*, (17) *kānaḍā*, (18) *gauḍamalhāra*, (19) *kedārā*, (20) *paṭamañjarī*, (21) *rāmakalī*, (22) *gāndhārī*, (23) *barāḍī*, (24) *kukubha*, (25) *kāmoda*, (26) *naṭa*, (27) *guṇakalī*, (28) *mādhavī*, (29) *deśa*, (30) *vibhāsa*, (31) *hāsa*, (32) *kāphī*, (33) *soraṭha*, (34) *īmana*, (35) *jayajayavantī*, and (36) *sāraṅga*.

---

1. *Aṣṭachāpīya Bhakti Saṅgīta (Havelī Saṅgīta) — Udbhava va Vikāsa* (author Śrī Campak Lāl Chabīladās Nāyak). This is mentioned on pages 116-17 of this book with the reference of book *Khaṭ-Ṛtu Vārtā*. Names of some *rāga*s and musical instruments (which are underlined) are not in vogue these days. Where and how these vanished, is a matter of research. In sequence of time some new names have come into force in the places of old names.

Number of instruments is also 36 — (1) *vīṇā*, (2) *muralī*, (3) *amṛta kuṇḍalī*, (4) *jalataraṅga*, (5) *madanabheri*, (6) *dhosā*, (7) *dundubhi*, (8) *niśāna*, (9) *nagāḍā*, (10) *śaṅkha*, (11) *ghaṇṭā*, (12) *muhacaṅga*,[2] (13) *sīṅgī*, (14) *khañjarī*, (15) *tāla*, (16) *mañjīrā*, (17) *khaḍatāla*, (18) *mahuvari*, (19) *thārī*, (20) *jhālara*, (21) *ḍhola*, (22) *ḍapha*, (23) *ḍimaḍima*, (24) *jhāñjha*, (25) *mṛdaṅga*, (26) *giḍagiḍī*, (27) *pināka*, (28) *rabāba*, (29) *jantra*, (30) *śahanāī*, (31) *śrīmaṇḍala*[3], (32) *sāraṅgī*, (33) *duvārī*, (34) *karatāla*, (35) *turahī*, and (36) *kinnarī*.

After poets of "Aṣṭa Chāpa" in the field of devotional music, the contribution of Svāmī Haridāsa of Vrindavana is notable. (Svāmī Haridāsa was the *guru* of famous musician, Tānsen, who was one of the *nava ratna*s of Moghul Emperor Akbar). He was the best poet, super musician and supreme Vaiṣṇava. Some words of his *Rāgamālā* are being mentioned here the *rāga*s changing in accordance to the change in time is miraculous —

'bhaura 'va' bhayo jāge jaga lāla ho aba 'rāmakalī' udai bhayo bhāna ॥
'guna kī kalī' guna pūrana pyārī kahā aba hota 'devagāna' ॥
dhruva ॥ (1 *devagāndhāra*)
bhayo 'vibhāsa' ābhāsa saba dekhiyata, calī jāūṅ 'torī' sunī le kāna ॥
'āsāna kari' tū apane prītama kī, 'soraṭha' samujhi le manahī mana jāna ॥ (2 *āsāvarī*)
'sāraṅga' nāma jāko tāke pāsa jāya ālī, 'naṭa' bhayo kahā kare abhimāna ॥
citavana citta 'puraba' -mukha baiṭhī, 'madhumāgha' mada bhayo taukūṅ āni ॥
ye krodha bhayo 'gaurī' kauna gunata teṅ, 'ī mana' kahā karaun kahā kahi bānī ॥

---

2. *murachaṅga* of these days is originally *muhacaṅga* (more meaningful name).
3. Is *svaramṇḍala* of these days actually? *śrīmaṇḍala*[1] (it is quite possible).

'kai dāruna' dukha miṭa gayo, 'kānhara' tero jīvana prāṇa ।
raina 'bihāya' gaī pyārī piya pāsa gaī, madana mohana piya ati hī sujāna ॥
calata 'hiṅḍola' sobhā lasata, 'aṅkamāla' bana ṭhana gahi pānī ॥
(3 *mālava*)
'haridāsa' ke svāmī śyāmā kuñja bihārī, 'lalita' carana cita dharūṁ dhyāna ॥

Again from the book *Aṣṭachāpīya*, composed by Caṁpak Lāl Nayak (pages 81-82):

It will be better if any musician would try to reconstruct it.[4]

Now let us listen or read, or listen and read one presentation of each of the eight *bhakta* poets-musicians. Let us look at the creation of the first devotional singer, skilful in speech and an erudite musician Śrī Kumbhanadāsa of Puṣṭimārga devotional music, i.e., "Havelī Music," *Rāga Vilāvala: Tāla Dhamāra* (still in vogue) —

sthāyī: sāñjha ke sāñce bola tihāre ॥
antarā: rajanī anata jāge nanda nandana, āye nipaṭa sakāre ॥1 ॥
sañcārī: ātura bhaye nīla paṭa oḍheṅ, pīre basana bisāre ॥
ābhoga: kumbhanadāsa prabhu govardhna dhara, bhale ju vacana pratipāre ॥2 ॥ — *Aṣṭachāpīya*, p. 131

The second poet is *bhakta* musician Sūradāsa Jī (it is said that he had composed 1 lakh 25 thousand *padas*.) Once, after saving the blind *bhakta* who was about to fall in a well, when Śrī Kṛṣṇa was about to return, the *bhakta* sung — *bāṅha chuḍāe jāta ho nibala jānike mohi* । *hiradeṅ teṅ jaba jāuge marda badauṅ main tohi*. Tānsen, the best singer of his time, said about Sūradāsa when he once saw a man restless —

---

4. The task is difficult due to changes in forms and tones of *rāgas* in a period of 500 years but efforts should be done.

kidhoṅ sūra ko sara lagyo, kidhoṅ sūra kī pīra ।
kidhoṅ sūra ko pada lagyo, tāteṅ dhunata sarīra ॥

The *padas* of Sūradāsa are generally marked with romance and comic elements.

The third *bhakta*, musician, devotional singer was Śrī Kṛṣṇa Dās Jī —

sthāyī: *mero mana giradhara chavi para aṭakyo* ।
antarā: *lalita tribhaṅgī aṅganī ūpara cali gayau tahāṅī ṭhaṭhakyo* ।
sañcārī: *sajala syāmaghana nīla barana hai, phiri cita anata na bhaṭakyo* ।
ābhoga: *kṛṣṇadāsa kiyo prāna nyauchāvara yaha tana jaga sira paṭakyo* ॥

— *Rāga Pūrabī*

The fourth musician of Aṣṭachāpa was Parmānanda Dāsa Jī who was initiated by Svāmī Vallabhācārya Jī. He sang before Guru Jī : *jiya kī sādha jiya meṅ rahī rī.* His *pada* was sung in *rāga Āsāvarī* — *māī rī kamala naina śyāma-sundara jhūlata hai palanā.* His another *pada* was sung in *rāga Bilāvala jasodā tere bhāga kī kahī na jāya* (even today it is sung in the same *rāga*).

The next musician was Govinda Svāmī who was initiated by Svāmī Viṭhalanāth Jī: a *tāla* of *rāga Īman* —

ṣaḍja, ṛṣabha, gāndhāra, sapta surani ।
madhama tīvara leta prapra tata tata tata horī ॥

The next musician and devotional singer was Chītasvāmī: His first composition in *pada* is available in *rāga Sāraṅga* —

je vasudeva kiye pūrana tapa, tehi pala phalita śrī vallabha deha ।
chītasvāmī giradharana śrī viṭṭhala tehi eī, eī, teī kachu na sandeha ॥

The seventh devotional singer was Śrī Caturbhuja Dāsa Jī who was the youngest son of the first devotional singer Śrī Kumbhana Dāsa Jī. His composition in *Sāraṅga rāga* is as under —

aisehu mohi kyon na sikhāvahu ।
'sāraṅga' rāga sarasa nandanandana saji sapta sura gāvahu ॥
tāna baṅdhāna sujāna sahaja meṅ bahuta anāgata lāvahu ॥
smṛti saṅgīta karo parimita tāhi teṅ atīta baḍhāvahu ॥
'caturbhuja' prabhu giradhara guṇa sāgara jo iha tuma janāvahu ।

The eighth and last musician and *bhakta* poet of this series was Śrī Nanda Dāsa Jī. Series of *Sāraṅga rāga* out of his three series of *rāgas* is as under —

(sthāī) *'sāraṅga' nainī rī kāheko liyo hai aiso māna* ।
(*antarā*) *'gauri' garaba chāṅḍi mila lāleṅ, mana, krama, vacana yāteṅ hota 'kalyāṇa'* ॥
(*sañcārī*) *jina haṭha kara rī 'naṭa' nāgara so māherī 'devagāna'* । (1 *devagāṅdhāra*)
(*ābhoga*) *muralī tāna 'kānharo' gāvana suna lai rī dai kāna* ॥
(*sancārī*-2) *raṅga raṅgīlī sudhara 'nāyikā' tū jina jiyameṅ 'aḍāna'*

(It is surprising that the name of *rāginī* is *nāyikā*)
(ābhoga-2) nandadāsa 'kedaro' karike yoṅ hī 'vihāī' gayo māna ।

After these examples there is a *dhruvapada* (*Cautāla*) in "*Pūrva Kalyāṇa* of Chītasvāmī which is the best example of Kānhā's love for cows —

āge gāya, pācheṅ gāya, ita gāya uta gāya, gobinda ko gāyana meṅ[5] *basabauī bhāvai* ।
gāyana ke saṅga dhāvai, gāyana meṅ sacu pāvai, gāyana kī khura-raja aṅga lapaṭāvai ॥
gāyana soṅ bṛja chāyau, vaikuṇṭha bisarāyau, gāyana ke heta giridhara teṅ uṭhāyau ॥
chītasvāmī giradhārī viṭṭhaleśa bapu dhārī, gvāriyā ko bheṣa dhareṅ gāyana meṅ āvai ॥

In the service and worship of the eight *yāmas*, the time limit of the eight poets was also ascertained. Paramānanda Dāsa

5. The word *gāyana* has been used as plural word of *gāya* (many cows) here, not in the meaning of singing a song.

delivered his music service at the time of *maṅgalā* (5 a.m. to 7 a.m.), Nanda Dāsa at he time of *Śṛṅgāra* (7 a.m. to 8 a.m.), Govinda Svāmī at the time of *Gvāla* (9 a.m. to 10 a.m.), Kumbhanadāsa Jī at the time of *Rājabhoga* (10 a.m. to 12 noon), Sūradāsa at the time of *Utthāpana* (3.30 p.m. to 4.30 p.m.), Caturbhuja Dāsa at the time of *Bhoga* (5 p.m.), Chītasvāmī at the time of evening prayer (6.30 p.m.) and Kṛṣṇadāsa Jī at the time of sleeping (7 p.m. to 8 p.m.). Service of Ṭhākura Jī was performed with *rāga* and *bhoga*. It continues to be performed in the same way at present and will probably be performed in the future also. The roots of these beliefs and traditions are as much deep and strengthening that the new Western culture could not destroy it. Even in the present age of science and technology, such powerful traditions continue uninterruptedly by virtue of deep devotion towards it. Rāma and Kṛṣṇa can never vanish from India's thoughts. Their service, and giving up of oneself to them, with utter faith is present and will be for ever.

From the geographical point of view it is accepted unanimously that "Havelī Music" is spread over Braja to Rajasthan, extending to Gujarat and also to Maharashtra. Regional languages have not been influenced by "Havelī Music." Its title name "Havelī Music" is in vouge since a hundred years. When a question arose as to under which title should the music of Puṣṭimārga in All India Radio, be broadcast, Gosvāmī Vallabharāya Jī of Moṭā temple in Sūrat (a famous Vaiṣṇava temple where Bāla Gopāla has been worshipped) suggested the name "Havelī Music." Thus, the name came into vogue. At present the devotional music, music of service and worship in Vaiṣṇava temples is famous with the title name, "Havelī Music."

After historical and geographical discussion we would discuss "Havelī Music" from the viewpoint of music. The devotional music which has been presented daily in the service of Ṭhākura Jī in east-west-north India is "Havelī Music."

Samāja Gāyana is also connected with Vaiṣṇava temples but it is sung at a fixed time and on a fixed occasion. The "Vaiṣṇavī Music" is the same "Havelī Music" which has been played at the time of eight different *darśana*s during service in the eight *yāma*s daily.

It is very natural that *Dhruvapada*, that is to say "Havelī Music," flourished in the temples and *Darabārī Dhrupada* flourished in the *darabāra*s (royal courts) of different kings, *nawāba*s and *bādaśāha*s are supplementary to each other. The genre *Khyāla* seems to be very much influenced by "Havelī Music" and "Darabārī Music." There are two examples. In 1955 I had learnt a *Vilambita Khyāla* in *rāga Kedār — banaṭhana kara jo cale* what charming words, what an eminent combination of tones! I was more surprised to see the same composition with complete *sthāyī, antarā, sañcārī, ābhoga* forms, in the book *Aṣṭachāpīya Bhakti Saṅngīta* on pages 325-26 with the impression (*mohara*) of Kīrtanācārya Śrī Nandadāsa Jī (with a little textual variant).[6] Honourable *Saṅgīta Mārtaṇḍa* Oṁkāranātha Ṭhākura's *Vilambita Khayāla* in *rāga Mālakauṅsa* is given in the aforesaid book on pages 68-99, with complete *Dhruvapada* (*sthāyī-antarā-sañcārī-ābhoga*) *svaralipi*. Name of the composer is the *Saṅgīta Samarāṭ* Tānsen.[7] There are 27 examples of this sort in this book. Apart from these are 42 such examples which

---

6. Rāga *kedāro* tāla *cautāla* (*dhruvapada*). This *pada* is mentioned on pages 325-26, along with sound script in the book of Śrī Campak Lal Jī.

   sthāyī *: banaṭhani kahā ju cale ho, aisī kauna mana bhāī,*
   sāṅvare salone kanhāī ।

   antarā *: mukha sauheṅ jaise dūja ko candā* ।
   chipa chipa deta dikhāī ॥1 ॥

   sañcārī *: bhale hī jāu neka ṭhāḍe rahoge* ।
   kina sautana aisī sīkha sikhāī ।

   ābhoga *: 'nandadāsa' prabhu aba na banegī* ॥
   nikāsī jāyegī ṭhakurāī ॥2 ॥

7. ***rāga***: *mālakauṅsa* ***tāla***: *cautāla* (*druvapada*) (*saṁpūrṇa svara lipi sahita*)
   sthāyī: *pīra na jānī ahopiya, dekhī tihārī aisī anokhī rīta (prīta)*
   antarā: *hamasoṅ avadhi badī, abala bilama rahe, kauna gāṅva kī yaha rīta* ॥1 ॥

→

explain the direct contact of Havelī Music to the *dhruvapada* singers in various *gharānā*s (Ḍāgara Gharānā and Mallika Gharānā, of Darabhaṅgā). The scripture of Dr. Selīna presents a comparative study of the three. Sometimes, name of the *rāga* has been same and sequence of tones (*loj*) has also been same, just as Prabhāta Bhairava sometimes name of the *rāga*s has been same but sequence of the tones are different, just as *Vibhāsa* (lustre) of Havelī Music is combined with pure *gha*. Sometimes sequence of the tones has been same but names of *rāga*s differ, as *Mālava, Bhūpa* of Havelī Music are in same tones. Even significance of the rhythms is also almost same in Havelī Music and *dhruvapada* of *gharānā*s. Havelī Music has remained music of devotion. Singing of *dhruvapada* consists predominantly of rhythm. Singing of *khyāla* is singing of tones these days. An appropriate conjunction of tone-rhythm-*pada* and accomplishing right, coordination of savour *rasa-bhāva-śāstra* are capable of making it "divine music." Beautifying aspects of tradition and experiments along with the judicious representation of old and new by *śāstra* can enrich as well as enhance the continuity of *rāga*-music.

It is an accepted fact that Havelī Music has three *gharānā*s — first Mathurā Gharānā, second Nāthadvārā (near Udaipur) Ghārānā, and the third Kiśanagaḍha (near Ajmer) Gharānā. Aim of all the three was same — service of Ṭhākura Jī. Often solo singing has been performed. Accompaniment of *pakhāvaja* is necessary. Other required musical instruments (in mordern age) are *hārmonium* and *mañjīrā*. Sometimes, there are more than one singer, more than two musicians and one leader accompanied by 5 to 10 co-singers.

It is a matter of pleasure that the writers from home and abroad have paid enough attention to Havelī Music, and made

---

→ ***sañcārī***: *tāre ginata mohe cāra juga bīte, kona ke bhavanani sidhāre ho mīta* ।

ābhoga: *'tānasena' ke prabhu aba na patyāūṅ, tumeṅ kari rākhoṅ rasarīta* ॥2॥

available adequate official awareness in the form of books and write-ups. Several audio cassettes and CDs are available in the market. There are two significant sound recordings. One of them is MAK, CD, 028, "La Tradition Lyrique du Dhruvpad" — "Nāth Dwārā Havelī Dhruvapad" Singer Pt. Girish Karya. The second is Śrī Viṭṭhala Dās Vāpodara's 10 audio cassettes titled as "Havelī Saṅgīta — Puṣṭimārgīya Saṅgīta Bhakti Saṅgīta." Limited to the temples and connected with worship and adoration, Havelī Music has always been away from any propaganda.

Paṇḍit Nāyak Jī has mentioned several sound scripts in his books alongwith a very good definition of the text. Havelī Music has been compared with other genre of music. Description of the applied *rāgas* (74 *rāgas* in 10 *thāṭas*), sense of rythms and words of medieval Aṣṭachāpīya series of *rāgas* have been found. The learners of Havelī Music should consider these scriptures as *Gītā*, *Bible* and *Koran*.

On the other hand, an Italian writer, Dr. Selina Theilaman, has written a book in English in two volumes titled *Viśvakoṣa* (Encyclopaedia). She lived in Mathura-Vṛndāvana and worked hard for this valuable task. Many photos, sound-scripts (Indian and staff notation), "Discography" (mention of sound recordings) and account of the printed material about "Vaiṣṇavī Music" included in her scriptures renders them invalubale. Dr. Selina was fortunate in receiving co-operation of the erudite scholar Ācārya Premabahana Jī.

Since this write-up mentions the "Contribution of Vaiṣṇavas to Kāśī," and "Place of Havelī Music in Kāśī," I would like to further add some more information. A write-up of Dr. Sima Gujarati was published in the edition of the year 1991 of *Dhruvapad Vārṣīkī* — not very early but in Saṁvat 1871 (AD 1823). Tilakāyat Śrī, Dāujī Mahārāja, influenced by "Śuddhādvaita Mārttaṇḍa" (a platform established by Puṣṭimārgīya Ācārya Vallabhajī in Varanasi) Śrī Giradhara Lal Jī got initiated with Gopāla *mantra*. In AD 1830 Gopāla temple

A Brief Introduction of Aṣṭachāp

Sr. No.	Name	Birth [Saṁvat]	Year of Initiation [Saṁvat]	Caste [Sakhā]	Name at Initiation	Permanent dwelling	Initiating Guru	Death [Saṁvat]
1.	Śrī Kumbhana Dās	1525	1556	Goravā Kṣatriya	Arjuna	Jamunavato	Śrī Vallabhācarya Jī	1640
2.	Śrī Sūrdāsa Jī	1535	1568	Sanāḍhya Brāhmaṇa	Kṛṣṇa	Pārasaulī	- do -	1640
3.	Śrī Kṛṣṇa Dāsa Jī	1553	1568	Kunavī Paṭel	Ṛṣabha	Villachu Kunḍa	- do -	1641
4.	Śrī Parmānanda Dāsa Jī	1550	1577	Kānyakubja Brāhmaṇa	Ḷoka	Surabhī Kunḍa	- do -	1636
5.	Śrī Govind Svāmī	1562	1592	Sanāḍhya Brāhmaṇa	Śrīdāmā	Kadam Khandi	Śrī Viṭṭhala Nāth Jī	1642
6.	Śrī Chīta Svāmī	1573	1592	Mathuriya Chaube	Sujana	Pūcharī	- do -	1642
7.	Śrī Caturbhuja Dāsa Jī	1587	1598	Goravā Kṣatriya	Viśala	Jamunāvato	- do -	1642
8.	Śrī Nanda Dāsa Jī	1590	1607	Sanāḍhya Brāhmaṇa	Bhoja	Mānasī Gaṅgā	- do -	1640

• On the basis of page numbers 115, 127 and 128 of the book *Aṣṭachāpīya Sangīt — Udbhav Aur Vikās* (*Havelī Sangīt*) (Author: Champak Lal-Chabil Das-Nayak).

was built — the followers of Vallabha are engrossed in service even today — simultaneously "Havelī Saṅgīta" came into existence. A deep concentration is needed for devotion of God and music is a single means for concentration and in it also mainly the *dhruvapada*. Connected with Havelī Music, a gem of Kāśī, initiated in *pakhāvaja gharānās* of Mahārāja Kuraū Singh, Mṛdaṅgācārya Mabhujī Mahāraja was born in 1903. Mabhujī's accompaniment on *pakhāvaja* with the singer of Havelī Music Paṇḍita Rāmnārāyaṇajī and Paṇḍita Govindarama Jī Kirtaniyā, in those days, used to be a delight. Paṇḍita Mabhujī had the knowledge of *dhruvapada-dhamāra*. He was a favourite disciple of Mahamana Madan Mohan Malaviyaji. Gayānācārya Paṇḍita Śiva Prasad Tripāṭhī was appointed professor of songs and Paṇḍita Mabhujī as professor of *pakhāvaja* and *tablā*.

Saṅgīta Mārttaṇḍa Paṇḍita Oṅkāranātha Ji Ṭhākura, established Sri Kala Sangit Bharati in 1950. After that the old system ended. Pt. Mabhujī had opened a school of music in "Raṇachoḍa Jī" temple of Kāśī where several students learnt singing and playing on *pakhāvaja*. Later, his disciple Pt. Sītārāmajī had run the school. With India's cultural capital Varanasi, three persons are connected with Havelī Saṅgīta, in the temple of Śrī Śaradavallabhā Beṭī Jī — Śrī Paṇḍita Śyāma Lāl Jī (singer), Pt. Rādhāvallabha Jī (*hārmonium* player) and Pt. Kṛṣṇa Dāsa Jī/Pt. Munnā Jī (*pakhāvaja* player). The three are presenting Havelī Music in the service of Ṭhākura Jī daily.[8] It is devotional singing-remembering of God.

8. The facts mentioned in this short write-up have been obtained from Dr. Urmila which are being mentioned below —
   (a) *Aṣṭachāpīya Bhakti Saṅgita — Udbhava aur Vikāsa* (*Havelī Saṅgīta*) Kīrtanācārya Ustad Śrī Campaklal, Chabīladās Nāyak, Ahmedabad: Aṣṭachāpa Saṅgīta Kalā Kendra
   (b) Dr. Selina Theilaman, *Musical Traditions of Vaiṣṇava Temples in Vraj*, Delhi: Sagar Printers.
   (c) Pt. Sri Syamdas's "Haveli Sangit" in *Dhruvapad Vārṣikī* (1991).
   (d) Dr. Sima Gujarati's, "Gopala Mandira ki gayana śailī evam Mṛdaṅgācārya sva. pan. Mabhujī Mahārāja: Saṁkṣipta paricaya," in *Dhruvapad vārṣikā* (1991).

12

Vaiṣṇava Texture of Kāśī

An Antiquarian Perspective

R.C. Sharma

Kāśī or Varanasi has been a stronghold of Saivism since times immemorial. At the same time it has been associated with other religions and sects which have contributed a lot in spreading the academic and spiritual glory of the city. Here we are concerned with its relation with Vaisnavism.

Nothing can definitely be said on the basis of the Vedic texts, although Rudra and Viṣṇu both are important gods. The epic literature does refer to Kāśī but the description is rather scanty. According to the *Vālmīki Rāmāyaṇa* Pururavas was the king of Kāśī[1] and at another place Puru, the son of Yayāti has been mentioned as ruler of Kāśī along with Pratiṣṭhāna.[2] The *Mahābhārata* has numerous references to Kāśī like the kidnapping of the three daughters of Kāśirāja, i.e., Ambā, Ambikā, and Ambālikā,[3] participation of the king of Kāśī in the Bhārata war in support of Pāṇḍavas[4] and burning of the city by Kṛṣṇa.[5] The early texts like the *Hiraṇyakeśi Gṛhyasūtra* assigned to about the fifth century BC, record the

---

1. *Vālmīki Rāmāyaṇa*, Uttara Kāṇḍa, 56.25.
2. *Ibid.*, 59.19.
3. *Mahābhārata*, Udyoga-Parva, 172.94.
4. *Ibid.*, *Gītā*, 1.5.
5. *Ibid.*, Udyoga-Parva, 47.40.

worship of Viṣṇu, Rudra, Skanda, Jvara and Kāśīśvara in Kāśī.[6] Jvara (fever) was probably deified due to its notorious and fatal impact.[7] Some of the Purāṇas observe that Kāśī was gifted to Śiva by Viṣṇu.[8] The period of these texts varies from about third century AD to the fourteenth century AD.

The figures and motifs as noticed on the finely carved ring stones recovered from Rājaghāṭ (Varanasi) appear to bear the Vaiṣṇava testimony and Lakṣmī is conspicuous, the *cakra* (disc) is also distinct. The entire shape of the composition with or without perforation in centre is circular. These have been assigned to the pre-Christian era.[9] There are some terracotta seals belonging to the Kuṣāṇa period — second century AD — on which *śrīvatsa* motif is seen. The other seals bear the name of Hariṣeṇa[10] and Kṛṣṇaṣeṇa and on the basis of these legends, Viṣṇu's association may be conjectured.

The practice continues in the Gupta period from the early fourth century AD. We do have some seals again from Rājaghāṭ preserved in Bharat Kala Bhavan on which the names given indicate their Vaiṣṇava nature. These are Bhāgavata, Haridāsa, Mādhava, Keśavavarmā, Haribhaṭṭa, Vallabha, Viṣṇumitra, etc. On the other hand, one seal depicts *śaṅkha* (conch) and *cakra* (disc) on a shrine. The Pusphasar seal illustrates a Viṣṇu temple and footprint of Viṣṇu.[11] We are well aware of the fact that the Gupta kings were *paramabhāgavata* (staunch devotee of Viṣṇu) and depiction of this deity and bearing his name must have naturally been popular, as Kāśī was the part of their territory. The recovery of the gigantic size statue of Kṛṣṇa

6. Hiraṇyakeśi *Gṛhya Sūtra*, 2.7 10.7.
7. Moti Chandra, *Kāśī Kā Itihāsa*, 1985, p. 160.
8. *Ibid.*, p. 31.
9. Pramod Chandra, 'The Cult of Śrī Lakshmī etc.' *Chhavi* I, 1971 pp. 146-47.
10. Moti Chandra, *op. cit.*, p. 71.
11. *Ibid.*, p. 95.

lifting Govardhana from Bakariakund near Jagatganj, Varanasi is a solid proof of the existence of Vaiṣṇava temple of the Gupta period at Varanasi. This remarkable statue is now displayed in the Bharat Kala Bhavan, Banaras Hindu University (*fig.* 12.1).[12]

The early Purāṇas were composed in this glorious period and some of these must have been written/re-written or edited in Varanasi, for example the *Kūrma Purāṇa* begins as a Vaiṣṇava treatise but later modified as Śaiva work. This indicates that there was a rivalry between the Saivism and Vaishnavism and the contents of the books were revised as per circumstances.

Beside the well-known Govardhanadhārī image as stated above, there are some other Vaiṣṇava specimens of Gupta period recovered from Varanasi and now housed in the Bharat Kala Bhavan. The important ones are as under :

1. A stele representing Yaśodā churning butter and child Kṛṣṇa trying to steal (No. 180, *fig.* 12.2). There are two other female figures in the background and these may be identified as *gopīs,* although the exact provenance is missing yet the sculpture hails from the city.[13]
2. An important pillar (No. 225) in the buff stone with an inscription of the reign of Buddhagupta, i.e., Gupta Era 159, corresponding to AD 478. The name of the donor is given Dāmasvāminī, whose father was Mārāvise and mother Sābhāti. The family belonged to Paravirika. The pillar is carved with the figure of Vāmana inside a niche. Another figure which is also seen in a niche is Narasiṁha. On the other side is a

12. T.K. Biswas and Bhogendra Jha, *Gupta Sculptures,* Bharat Kala Bhavan 1985, p. 37, fig. 9.
13. *Ibid.,* p. 38, fig. 10

female figure holding a lotus on the basis of which she may be identified as Lakṣmī. This was found from Rājaghāṭ.[14]

3. Another Viṣṇu pillar (No. 29) bears an inscription in *śaṅkhalipi* and should be assigned to the fifth century AD. In its four niches in four different directions, are seen four armed Viṣṇu with lotus, conch-shell and club, four armed Narasiṁha holding lotus, conch, club and wheel with a *vaijayantīmālā*. Varāha is seen lifting *pṛthivī* and the fourth niche consists of two-armed Kapila with matted hair, staff and rosary. The findspot is mentioned as Varanasi only.[15]

4. The male deity (No. 23973) although badly mutilated can be identified as Viṣṇu on the basis of *vaijayantīmālā,* a short loin cloth, royal crown and carvings. The findspot is Varanasi.[16]

5. There is four-armed Viṣṇu seated on lotus, wearing a crown and long garland. Traces of *gadā* and *cakra* are also seen (No. 169561). The figure comes from Sārnāth.[17]

6. There is an interesting male bust with locks of hairs and a flute in the left hand on the basis of which one is inclined to identify him as the figure of Kṛṣṇa or Veṇugopāla (No. 508). This was also recovered from the city of Varanasi.[18]

7. There is a bust of Viṣṇu with halo, crown traces of *vaijayantīmālā* and ear-rings (No. 427). The findspot is recorded as Varanasi.[19]

---

14. *Ibid.*, p. 39, fig. 14.
15. *Ibid.*, p. 40, fig. 13.
16. *Ibid.*, p. 43.
17. *Ibid.*
18. *Ibid.*, p. 42.
19. *Ibid.*, p. 43.

8. Head probably of Viṣṇu (No. 23976) with a crown, from Varanasi.[20]
9. A slab depicting Viśvarūpa Viṣṇu in which a number of divine figures are carved (No. 152). This also comes from the city.[21]
10. A very interesting slab which may be dated in sixth century AD represents the *Rāmāyaṇa* scene and particularly the erection of bridge at Rāmeśvaram. Rāma, Lakṣmaṇa, Sugrīva, Hanumān and other figures are quite clear. Its findplace is again Varanasi[22] (*fig.* 12.3).

All these sculptures are shaped in the Chunār sandstones and should have been the products of the Sarnath School in Gupta period. Of course, the Buddha images of this period bespeak the zenith of art of Varanasi or Sārnāth, yet the other sculptures and particularly, the Vaiṣṇava sculptures as discussed, are also beautiful specimens. Their discovery in Varanasi and adjoining region certainly suggests the construction of one or more Viṣṇu temples in Kāśī. Incarnations, *līlās* of Kṛṣṇa and Rāma point to the fact that Vaishnavism was gaining popularity in the seat of Saivism under the care of the Bhāgavata Gupta rulers. Besides Bharat Kala Bhavan, there may be some other stray remains which should hint to the Vaiṣṇava leanings in Kāśī. As per epigraphic records a Viṣṇu temple was constructed in the post-Harṣa period by a king named Prakaṭāditya and the temple was called Muradviṣa.[23]

The process of spread of Vaishnavism in Kāśī not only continued but also accelerated in the reign of Gahaḍavāla rulers, i.e., between the eleventh and thirteenth centuries. They

20. *Ibid.*, p. 44.
21. *Ibid.*, p. 41, fig. 16.
22. *Ibid.*, p. 39, fig. 11.
23. J.H. Fleet, *Gupta Inscriptions*, p. 284.

were followers of Vaishnavism but also respected Saivism.[24] The temple of Ādikeśava is known by their inscriptions. Accordingly, the copper-plate of Jayacandra states that he gifted thirty two villages to five hundred brāhmaṇas and got himself initiated as the devotee of Kṛṣṇa.[25] Some other Vaiṣṇava temples also find mention in the documents of Govindacandra. When a house was gifted to Mahattakadāyin its boundary wall had three Śaiva and one Vaiṣṇava shrines. The latter was dedicated to deity Indramādhava.[26]

It appears that due to some abnormal ritual practices in Saivism and Buddhism in the medieval period the masses had started avoiding these sects and were prepared to embrace a way of life or a philosophy which propagated the pure devotion and was not indulged in obnoxious activities. The negative force of Tāntric cult provided a commensurate atmosphere for propagation of Vaishnavism on one hand and also for reforming Saivism on the other. The Buddhism was declining fast under the similar practices of Vajrayāna and it became almost extinct from the northern India and particularly in the region of Varanasi. The two works of Gahaḍavāla period namely *Prabodhacandrodaya*[27] by Kṛṣṇa Miśra and *Kalā-Vilāsa*[28] by Kṣemendra furnish ample evidence of the prevailing Tantric corruption in Saivism and Buddhism in Kāśī. The city fell to the Muslim invaders under the leadership of Mohammad Ghori in 1194 and the Gahaḍavāla king Jayacandra was defeated and killed in the battle.[29]

The late Medieval period is known for the arrival of a number of Vaiṣṇava saints to Kāśī from distant quarters of

---

24. Moti Chandra, *op. cit.*, p. 138.
25. *Epigraphia Indica,* 14, pp. 197-200.
26. *Ibid.*, 4, pp. 124-26.
27. Prabodha Chandrodaya, *Act* III, verse 13-15.
28. *Kalā Vilāsa,* 1.86-87, 5.40 and 9.66.
29. Moti Chandra, *op. cit.*, p. 122.

the country. Among them the well known personalities are Rāmānanda, Caitanya (Gauḍīya), Nānaka and Vallabha (Puṣṭi). Kabīra belonged to Kāśī and Tulasī, although came from Rajapur, Bāndā, yet spent most of his life in Kāśī.[30] The followers of Nimbārka also graced the city. The contribution of these saintly scholars is enormous and that of Tulasīdāsa[31] through his works *Rāmacaritamānasa* and *Vinayapatrikā* is certainly outstanding. The important establishments are Gopāla Mandir, Kabīramaṭha, Bindumādhava temple, Mahāviṣṇu temple, etc. The ancient *yakṣa pūjā* gradually gave way to Vīrapūjā, Bhairava and Mahāvīra (Hanumān) *pūjā,* the last dominated all being Vaiṣṇava in nature with great public impact.

This was the period when India was repeatedly attacked by the invaders who not only destroyed temples but also mutilated images. All the sects had to face this calamity separately or jointly. Both Saivites and Vaishnavites were now engaged in protecting themselves and their religious edifices, forgetting their mutual sectarian competition and rivalry. Kāśī which housed hundreds of temples and shrines was the natural target of the iconoclastic forces. In this dark era the only option was to meditate on Almighty for His grace. The Tāntric practices of Saivism became redundant and devotion (*bhakti*) to deity whether Śiva or Viṣṇu, gained momentum. Much of the architectural, artistic and religious heritage was devastated and lost. The society, however, realised that the real weakness was in the misconduct and wrong rituals followed in the religion.

The sectarian clashes became rare and an environment of eclectism and harmony surfaced. Both Saivism and Vaishnavism progressed and flourished together in Kāśī and continue till date. We often notice Vaiṣṇava scenes on the Śaiva

---

30. *Ibid.*, pp. 190-92.
31. *Ibid.*, pp. 205-7.

temples and the Śaiva illustrations in the Vaiṣṇava religious places. The Lakṣmīnārāyaṇa temple and Raghurājeśvara temple both situated at Bhonslaghāṭ are notable citations. To avoid sectarian clash the *pañcadevopāsanā* tradition, which had the origin in the early *vyūha* or composite images, became the norm of the Hindu society and the post-Mogual circumstances prepared the fertile ground in Kāśī for the worship of different gods under one roof. Naturally, both the major sects, viz., Saivism and Vaishnavism came closer. There are several Vaiṣṇava shrines adjoining the famous Viśvanātha and Annapūrṇā temples.

The family deity of the founders of *Jñāna Pravāha* is Śrī Kṛṣṇa but Smt. Bimla Poddar decided to settle at Varanasi and established this cultural institution just on the bank of Gaṅgā with the grace of Lord Śiva. The introductory verse spells out the sentiments.[32] The devotion to Rādhā-Kṛṣṇa continues in the abode of Śiva and the seminar on the *Vaiṣṇava Contribution to Kāśī* unfolds the same mystery of strength in harmony. While former due to its deeper roots dominates, the latter is mainly respected through literatures and *līlā*s. This is the reason that the *Rāmacaritamānasa* is the most popular book among the masses and the same is the case with *rāma rāma* being more favourite than *jai śaṅkara* or *namaste* in the country side.

Mānasamandir (near Durgājī) in which the entire Mānasa is inscribed on the marble walls, is now an important landmark of Kāśī. The International Śrī Kṛṣṇa Consciousness (ISKCON) has been propagating Vaishnavism or Bhagavatism throughout the world and Kāśī is gradually developing as its centre. *Rathayātrā* of Jagannātha is their remarkable ceremony in public view and the publications are also attractive. Besides, there is an old temple of Jagannātha near Assī with a huge campus

32. *prasādād viśvanāthasya kāśyaṁ bhāgīrathī taṭe* ।
vṛddhirjñānapravāhe syāt saṁskṛteścānuśīlane ॥

but under precarious condition. Some Vaiṣṇava *līlās* on *ghāṭas* cater to a good number of people. It must be rewarding to note that *Jñāna Pravāha* possesses an important illustrated manuscript of AD 1736 titled as *Haricaritra.* It contains more than 400 illustrations in the folk style of paintings of Varanasi. This is probably the earliest text of its type.

13

Viṣṇu in the Art of Kāśī

Maruti Nandan Prasad Tiwari & Pramod Giri

KĀŚĪ as we all know was divided mainly as Śiva Kāśī and Viṣṇu Kāśī.[1] We propose to discuss in the present paper the *ekala* images of Viṣṇu found from different places in Kāśī. These images belong mainly to a period from about seventh century to thirteenth century AD and even beyond that. The paper aims at discussing mainly those images (about 10 in number) which are scattered over or are preserved in the temples, sometimes even in worship. The stylistic and iconographic features of *ekala* images of Viṣṇu will be discussed here which are found in continuity from about seventh century AD and which represent different stylistic features of pre-Pratihāra, Pāla, Pratihāra, Candella, Kaḷacūri and Gahaḍavāla periods.

The images of different styles, though meagre in number, suggest that Kāśī was almost equally important for the Vaiṣṇavas who took pilgrimage to this place and paid their homage to Lord Viṣṇu through the carving and installation of images. These images, besides revealing the political sway of different dynasties, also present Kāśī as a great centre of pilgrimage and cultural confluence. Kāśī atleast by the time of the Gupta rulers was having some Vaiṣṇava temples as suggested by the findings of huge Govardhanadhārī Kṛṣṇa

---

1. *Nārada* and *Vāmana Purāṇa*, *Tristhali-setu*, p. 216; Kāśī Khaṇḍa of *Skanda Purāṇa*, 61, 207-9.

image from Bakariā Kuṇḍa near Alaipura-Varanasi City station on G.T. Road which belonged possibly to fifth century AD.[2]

One of the earliest known Viṣṇu figures from Kāśī is carved on a Caumukhī image of about seventh century AD found at Lolārka Kuṇḍa near Assī. It shows the figures of Viṣṇu, Umā-Maheśvara, Durgā and Gaṇeśa on four sides. The figure of four-armed Viṣṇu standing in *samabhaṅga* with placid and pleasing face shows the continuation of the later Gupta style (*fig.* 13.1) The long *vanamālā* (a typical feature of Viṣṇu image) and a small decorated *kirīṭa-mukuṭa* and also the small face are all in Pre-Gurjara Pratihāra style and hence the image could well be dated to Harṣa's time. The rounded plasticity and grace are all superb. Viṣṇu holds mace, *mātuliṅga* (fruit), conch and disc in the style of the Gupta images. Instead of holding the attributes in hands Viṣṇu places his hands on mace and disc, which again was an early feature.

Another image of four-armed Viṣṇu in typical Gahaḍavāla style of twelfth century AD is now preserved in the premises of Śuṣkeśvara temple of Sukulpura near Khojwan (Durgakunda) (*fig.* 13.2). The image though badly mutilated with head being completely lost is important from the view point of iconography. Viṣṇu with *kaustubhamaṇi* symbol on chest and long *vanamālā* stands in *samabhaṅga* on *triratha* pedestal. The composition of the *parikara* and the modelling of the figure are graceful and animated. The moderate body though not much slim has the grace and dignity of Viṣṇu who is the cause of preservation of the entire world.

The image also exhibits two such features which are commonly found in north Indian Viṣṇu images. These features pertain respectively to the renderings of incarnatory forms of Viṣṇu in the *parikara* and also to the rendering of the figures of

---

2. Anand Krishna, "The Gupta Style of Sculpture from the City of Banaras," *Rūpa-Pratirūpa* (Alice Boner Commemoration Volume), New Delhi, pp. 87-95.

four-armed Brahmā and Viṣṇu in diminutive forms at the two top ends of the image. The presence of Brahmā and Śiva with Viṣṇu (being the principal deity) is suggestive of the entire process of Creation, Preservation and Dissolution (*sṛṣṭi, sthiti* and *vilaya*) controlled by the trinity. It is quite interesting that the figures are in order, first comes Brahmā, the Creator, then Viṣṇu in the centre as the principal deity and at last Śiva, the cause of dissolution. Of the ten incarnatory forms only nine could be identified, these are Matsya, Kūrma, Nṛvarāha, Vāmana, Rāma (with bow and arrow), Balarāma (with snake canopy), Nṛsiṁha, Kalki (riding on horse) and Buddha.

However, Viṣṇu holds in his surviving lower left hand the principal *āyudha cakra*. The presence of *garuḍa* in human form on left flank is also worth noting. *Garuḍa* with garland of snake as usual shows snakes in his hands.

The iconographic features of *ekala* Viṣṇu images under the name Viṣṇu, Vāsudeva or even Para-Vāsudeva are enunciated in several texts and the Purāṇas, according to which the four-armed Viṣṇu with *srīvatsa* mark on chest and decked with *kaustubhamaṇi, kirīṭa-mukuṭa* and *vanamālā* is accompanied by *garuḍa vāhana*. The *Bṛhatsaṁhitā* of Varāhamihira (sixth century AD) conceives Viṣṇu as two, four and eight armed which testifies that by the sixth century AD. Viṣṇu was visualized in a variety of forms. It may be noted that in Kāśī and even at other prolific centres like Osiāñ and Khajurāho Viṣṇu in *ekala* form is usually shown mainly with four hands and as standing in *samabhaṅga* with *garuḍa vāhana*, shown in a human form with snakes around his head, neck and even in hands. The *Bṛhatsaṁhitā* envisages *abhaya-mudrā* and mace for right hands while the corresponding left ones show conch and disc.[3] Another text of the same period the *Viṣṇudharmottara Purāṇa* describes Viṣṇu in the name of Vāsudeva who is adorned with usual ornaments and is *sudarśana* (good looking) in appearance.

---

3. *Bṛhatsaṁhitā*, 57.31-35.

It makes detailed description of the *ekala* Viṣṇu image and prescribes lotus and conch in upper right and left hands while the lower hands of Viṣṇu are placed on the heads of *gadādevī* (on right) and *cakra puruṣa* (on left).[4] The rendering of *āyudha Puruṣas*, so popular during the Gupta period, was subsequently carried on during the Pratihāra, Candella and even Pāla period, a few examples of which are found from Kāśī also.

The description of the four-armed image of Viṣṇu found in the *Agni Purāṇa*[5] (eighth-ninth centuries AD) also gives the name Para-Vāsudeva for such images. Viṣṇu, according to the text holds disc and lotus in right hands while the left hands carry conch and mace. Interestingly, the figures of Śrī and Puṣṭi bearing respectively lotus and *vīṇā* are also to be shown on two flanks of Vāsudeva. It may be remembered that figures of Viṣṇu with Śrī and Puṣṭi are mainly found from eastern India, a few examples of which are also known from Kāśī.

Two important observations may be made here on the basis of the texts. First, the four-armed independent images of Viṣṇu may also be identified as Vāsudeva. Second, the texts perhaps do not prescribe the rendering of the incarnatory forms of Viṣṇu in the *parikara* which are found invariably in the images of Viṣṇu atleast from about *c.* eighth-ninth century AD.[6]

The Kardameśvara temple near Kandawa village is perhaps the only ancient surviving temple of Kāśī which belongs to the Gahaḍavāla period and is datable approximately to twelfth century AD. The temple is dedicated to Śiva but in keeping with the non-sectarian character of the Indian temples this temple also contains in its facade niches the figures not only

4. *Viṣṇudharmottara Purāṇa*, 85.1-18.
5. *Agni Purāṇa* 44.47-49.
6. Kamal Giri, Maruti Nandan Tiwari, and Vijay Prakash Singh, *Kāśī ke Mandir aur Mūrtiyāñ*, Varanasi, 1997, pp. 48-64.

of four-armed Vāsudeva but also of Vāmana, Varāha, Nṛsiṁha and Balarāma (along with Śakti). The *samabhaṅga* Vāsudeva image shown with *garuḍa vāhana* and *kirīṭa-mukuṭa* reveals stiffness in body (*fig*. 13.3). The four-armed Vāsudeva bears *varadākṣa,* mace, disc and conch. It appears that although the *Viṣṇudharmottara Purāṇa* and *Agni Purāṇa* prescribe lotus in one of the four hands of Vāsudeva yet in sculptural examples from Kāśī and elsewhere one hand is usually known in *varada* or *abhaya-mudrā* (sometimes with *varadākṣa*) to suggest the unceasing compassionate grace of God for the devotees. This also suggests the bearing of the *Bṛhatsaṁhitā* conceiving four-armed Viṣṇu as showing *abhaya-mudrā* with one of his hands.

A magnificent ninth or early tenth century image of four-armed *samabhaṅga* Viṣṇu can be seen in the Trilocana Mahādeva temple at Matsyodarī (now Machodarī) (*fig*. 13.4). The figure distinctly reveals the matured Pratihāra features in terms of slim and graceful body, plasticity and beautiful and light ornaments. The image may well be compared with Pratihāra figures from Kanauj. Here also Vāsudeva carries mace, disc and conch in three hands while the remaining one hand is in *varada-mudrā*. The rendering of the incarnatory forms of Viṣṇu in the *parikara* reveals compositional elegance which includes figures of Matsya, Kūrma, Varāha, Vāmana, Rāma, Balarāma and Nṛsiṁha.

Typical Pāla examples of Vāsudeva images are found from Gabhastīśvara temple (Viśvanātha Gali) and Bharata Kala Bhavan. The example of the Gabhastīśvara temple represents four-armed Vāsudeva as standing in *samabhaṅga* and bearing conch, disc and mace. The representation of disc and conch as *āyudha Puruṣa*s along with the figures of fly-whisk bearing Śrī and Vīṇā-dhāriṇī Puṣṭi are the features which were shown in the Pāla sculptures. The stone also is a black basalt one. The slim body, decoration of ornaments and *parikara* and stele are all typical Pāla. These images reveal that in Kāśī the Vāsudeva Viṣṇu images are carved mainly on the basis of the tradition of the early texts like *Bṛhatsaṁhitā* and *Viṣṇudharmottara* and *Agni Purāṇas.*

Another interesting image of four-armed Vāsudeva is preserved in the Kāśī Maṭha Saṁsthān at Brahmā Ghāṭ (*fig.* 13.5). The delineation of foliages, stele, *parikara* composition, stone and the presence of the figure of Śrī and Puṣṭi are all in Pāla style but the modelling of the Śrī-mūrti (main figure) of Vāsudeva with volume and without Pāla delicacy reminds of Pratihāra-Candella style. Thus the present image is an outcome of the fusion of different styles. Vāsudeva standing in *samabhaṅga* shows as usual — clockwise — *varada-mudrā,* mace, disc and conch.

Two other examples of Vāsudeva images are worth mentioning which belong to the Candella and Kaḷacūri styles. The image with rounded plasticity, volume and ornaments typical of Candella images is being worshipped in the twentieth-century Rāma temple situated in Mānasarovara Muhallah (locality) (*fig.* 13.6). The *kirīṭa-mukuṭa* and other ornaments are all in Candella style of tenth century AD. The transparent *dhotī* with design, small face and comparatively bigger eyes and attributes are all pleasing and in Candella style. The image is completely preserved. Vāsudeva standing in *samabhaṅga* shows (clock-wise) conch, lotus, disc and mace. The figure of *garuḍa* is carved in human form. As usual the top ends of *parikara* exhibit the seated figures of Brahmā (with *sruk* and manuscript) and Śiva (with trident and snake) which were shown mostly in Candella and Gahaḍavāla images.

The eleventh-century beautiful image of Vāsudeva with all the four hands being broken is lying unshaded in the courtyard of Dvārakādhīśa temple at Śaṅkudhārā (*fig.* 13.7). Vāsudeva is adorned with a number of necklaces and tall *kirīṭa-mukuṭa* carved profusely, with dexterity. The benign and oval face has a divine look. The exquisitely carved image is hewn out of blackstone and is undoubtedly one of the masterpieces of Kaḷacūri art. Some portion of mace of Viṣṇu is also visible. The figures of worshippers and attendants along with Bhūdevī with snake conopy are vibrant and profusely bejewelled.

Thus, the Vāsudeva-Viṣṇu images from Kāśī show different art styles which developed in succession with overlappings in Kāśī which was an equally important place of pilgrimage for the Vaiṣṇavas. The images bear testimony to this. The images also suggest that they were carved on the basis of the texts and they do reveal some distinct regional iconographic features.

14

Vaiṣṇava Images of Kāśī

Kamal Giri

A CONTINUAL current of the confluence of Indian cultural heritage could be seen from the centuries before Christ in the city of Kāśī. Temples of different *dharma*s are still proof of this fact. The same city has been the working place of many saints or thinkers like Buddha, Mahāvīra as well as Rāmānanda, Śaṅkarācārya, Tulasīdāsa, Vivekananda. In the early medieval period Kāśī was a rich city from the viewpoint of temples and cultural heritage. Unfortunately, it has been ruined by the repeated Muslim attacks. We can see medieval and earlier remains of temples and many unknown, scattered images made in regional styles and eminent from the viewpoint of art, walking on the roads, narrow streets and ghats in Kāśī even today.

These images manifest the art of sculpture in Kāśī and are datable from Gupta period to twentieth century. The images belonged to Brahmā, Buddha, Jaina and Loka Dharmas and these are the proof of this fact that a current of the art of sculpture was running in the nearby city (Kāśī) of the world famous Sarnath School.

Kāśī has been assumed the prominent centre for adoration of Śiva but it has also been mentioned as a seat of Viṣṇu in Purāṇas.[1] Reference of images of Nārāyaṇa, Śeṣaśāyī as well

---

1. *Nārada Purāṇa, Vāmana Purāṇa, Tristhali Setu,* Page 216.

as *avatāra*s of Viṣṇu like Matsya (fish), Kūrma (turtle), Kṛṣṇa, Paraśurāma, Rāma, Buddha have been found in Kāśī.[2] These are evidences of ancient tradition of Vaiṣṇava worship in Kāśī.

In this write-up an effort has been made for the distinction of the Vaiṣṇava images from the individual images of Kāśī.[3] In Vaiṣṇava images apart from the individual Viṣṇu images; of Nṛsiṁha, Nṛsiṁha-Lakṣmī, Jagannātha, Śeṣaśāyī, Viṣnu-Lakṣmī, Kṛṣṇa (Gopāla-Kṛṣṇa, Veṇu-Gopāla, Radhā-Kṛṣṇa, lifting of Govardhana in the views of *Kṛṣṇalīlā*, depiction of *Cīraharaṇa* (removing of the *sārī* of Draupadī) and grazing the cows, etc., are notable, and in forms of *avatāra*s images of Matsya (fish), Kūrma (turtle), Balarāma, Rāma, Paraśurāma, etc., have been found. These images can be seen in different temples, *maṭha*s, *akhāḍā*s, *maḍhi*s, *ghāṭa*s on Gaṅgā banks in Kāśī and also in different areas of the city. Kāśī has been ruled by several royal families such as Gupta, Maukharī, Pāla, Pratihāra, Rāṣṭrakūṭa, Candela, Kaḷacūri, Gahaḍavāla. All of those families have contributed in the art of sculpture. For this reason the influence of regional sculptural styles in the medieval images of Kāśī is marked.

Several Vaiṣṇava temples were built in Kāśī out of which Ādīkeśava group of temples at Keśava Ghāṭa (seventeenth-fifteenth centuries) consecrated in the times of Marāṭhās. Lakṣmī-Nārāyaṇa temple (AD 1795) at Bhoṅsalā Ghaṭ, Dvārakādhīśa temple at Śaṅkudhārā, Bālā Jī temple at Bālāghāṭa, Gopāla Baḍī (eighteenth century) at Pāṇḍey Ghat, Lakṣmī-Nārāyaṇa temple (nineteenth century) at Assī Ghat, Rāma temple (twentieth century) at Saṅkaṭmocana are notable.

Apart from these temples Pañcagaṅgā Ghat of Kāśī has been a prominent centre for Vaiṣṇava adoration since fourteenth century AD where splendid appearances of Viṣṇu-

---

2. *Kāśī Khaṇḍa*, 61, 207-09.
3. *Kāśī kī Ekal Viṣṇu Mūrtiyān*, commented by Prof. Marutinandan Tiwari, Art History Department, B.H.U.

Rāma, Sītā and Lakṣmaṇa have been much popular under the impact of Vaiṣṇava Dharamācārya Rāmānanda (fourteenth century AD). In the same region *Bindu mādhava* temple was also built. Vaiṣṇava Maṭhas of Kāśī have also contributed distinctly in diffusion of Vaiṣṇava faith and art. Among these notable ones are: Nāṛsiṁha Cauka Maṭha (Gaḍhavāsī Ṭolā), Rāmatāraka Maṭha (Durgā Ghat) Kāśī Maṭha Sansthān (Brahmā Ghat), Śrī Maṭha (Pañchagaṅgā Ghat), Tailaṅga Svāmī Maṭha (Pañcagaṅgā Ghat), Loṭa Tīlā Maṭha (Īśvargaṅgī). In these *maṭhas* images of Nṛsiṁha (stone, five metals), Kṛṣṇa, Rādhā-Kṛṣṇa, Veṇu-Gopāla, Gopāla-Kṛṣṇa, Bindu Mādhava, Sākṣī Gopāla, Rāma-Jagnnātha, etc., can be seen.[4] Out of these, some Vaiṣṇava images are the best examples of Indian art and assigned to ninth-tenth centuries from the viewpoint of time.

Study of Vaiṣṇava images in Kāśī begins from the collection of Bharat Kala Bhavan, Banaras University, Varanasi. In this collection a grand image of Kṛṣṇa holding Govardhana, found in Bakariyā Kuṇḍa, assigned to Gupta period (fourth-fifth centuries) is notable. Even though the image size is quite large, the expression of adolescent Kṛṣṇa is manifested through impressions of face, hair style and Baghanakhā worn on the neck. Among other Vaiṣṇava images of Gupta period in this collection, images of Rāmakathā, Kṛṣṇalīlā, Nṛsiṁha and a pillar combined with four faces found at Rājaghāṭa assigned to the ruling period of Budhagupta are significant. On this pillar, images of *sthānaka* Viṣṇu as well as Viṣṇu's *avatāra* Vāmana, Nṛsiṁha and Varāha are notable.[5]

The tradition of worship of *pañcāyatana* (five gods) has been given special importance in Kāśī. As a result images

---

4. Pramod Giri, *Kāśī Kī Vāstukalā: Maṭh Evaṃ Havelī ke sandarbha mein*, Art and History department, Banaras University, Varanasi.
5. Anand Krishna, "The Gupta style of sclupture from the city of Banāras," *Rūpa Prathirūpa* (*Alice Commemoration Volume*), New Delhi, p. 87-95.

representing different appearances of Śiva as well as Viṣṇu, Sūrya, Gaṇeśa, Śakti were built in the temples. Among these images, apart from the single images, there are images of Lakṣmī-Nārāyaṇa and Nṛsiṁha too. Generally, these images are assigned to eighteenth to twentieth centuries. Apart from *pañcāyatana* temples examples of some *pañcāyatana* Śiva Lingas and Caumukhī (four faces) are also found which affirmed the single appearance of Viṣṇu as well as his appearance as Varāha. Among such examples Caumukhī image combined with single Viṣṇu, assigned to about seventh century, made in Gurjar-Partihāra style, consecrated at Lolārka Kuṇḍa and *pañcāyatana* Śivaliṅga at Rāmnagar fort are notable. In the imge of Lolārka Kuṇḍa a beautiful melodious proportion of the parts of body, and club and wheel in the hands of Viṣṇu remind of Gupta style.[6] In the image of Rāmnagar, assigned to ninth century presence of Viṣṇu is revaled as Nara-Varāha.

Although, there has been dominance of Viṣṇu's individual *sthānaka* images made in regional styles in Kāśī, the sculptures depicting his other forms, Vāmana, Balarāma and other *avatāra*s are also significant. An image of Balarāma combined with seven fangs along with Śakti (*fig.* 14.2), assigned to about twelfth century, is embellished under a *pīpal* tree in Gayaghat Muhallā.[7] People worship it in the name of Śītalā at present. Another image of Balarāma along with Śakti at Kardameśvara temple, Kandavā is requiring attention. Balarāma is depicted in embracing pose having cup, plough and pestle. An image of Balarāma probably made in thirteenth century is embellished in Yogeśvara temple. The image of Vāmana *avatāra* (thirteenth century) can be seen at Kardameśvara temple, Rāmeśvara

6. Marutinandan Tiwari and Kamal Giri, "A unique Caumukhī image from Varanasi," *V.K. Thapar Commemoration Volume*.
7. Adoption of somewhat slanting posture can be seen in other contemporary images, mainly in the images of Umā-Maheśvara. It seems that it is an individual characteristic of the images of Kāśī of those times.

temple and in Viśvanātha street. A singnificant image of Viṣṇu's *avatāra* Nṛsiṁha along with Śakti built in black stone, assigned to tenth-eleventh centuries is seen in Hanumān temple in Rājmandira Muhallā.[8] The image of Lakṣmī is smaller than the image of Nṛsiṁha. Image of Lakṣmī-Nṛsiṁha is also established in Jñānakeśava temple at Ādikeśava Ghat whereas individual image of Nṛsiṁha is present in Kāmeśvara temple, Gayaghat. Images of Nṛsiṁha *avatāra* could also be seen in the *pañcāyatana* temples in Kāśī. There is an image combined with four hands in Khaḍga Vināyaka temple in which Nṛsiṁha can be seen tearing the stomach of Hiraṇyakaśipu. An image is present in the museum of Bharat Kala Bhavan depicting Kūrma (tortoise) *avatāra* assigned to tenth century in which a small shape of Viṣṇu is manifesting from the mouth of Kūrma (tortoise). Images manifesting *avatāra*s of Viṣṇu could be seen in Raghurājeśvara and Lakṣmī-Nārāyaṇa temples, among which there are several images of Matsya (fish) *avatāra*.

There is an abundance of Lakṣmī-Nārāyaṇa images among Viṣṇu images in Kāśī which have been given forms of *pañcāyatana* temples and else. Images of Lakṣmī-Nārāyaṇa in embracing pose can be seen in the Śiva temples situated at Agastya- kuṇḍa and Ḍuṇḍhirāja street. An image of this sort is fixed in the Maḍhī of Late Baburam Ghatiya at Durgā Ghat. Several images of Śeṣaśāyī shape are also found. These images can be seen at the banks of Lakṣmīkuṇḍa pond (eleventh century AD), at the stairs of Brahma Ghat fixed in the wall of Tātyā Paṭavardhan's house situated at Durgā Ghat (eighteenth century), Raghurājeśvara and Lakṣmī-Nārāyaṇa temple (Bhoṅsalā Ghat), and Durgā temple, Rāmnagar. In the image of Lakṣmī-Kuṇḍa Lakṣmī is shown massaging the feet of Viṣṇu

8. It may be pointed out that several images having similarity to Pāla-Sena style, carved in black stone and assigned to tenth-eleventh centuries have been found in the temples and *maṭha*s of Kāśī. An example can also be seen in Bharat Kala Bhavan Museum.

lying in easy posture whereas image of Brahmā is carved on the navel and Madhu-Kaiṭabha below the navel. Apart from Garuḍa, below the shape of Śeṣanāga two horses are carved. In the images of Durgā Ghāṭa figures of *avatāras* of Viṣṇu such as Matsya (fish), Kūrma (tortoise), Varāha, Nṛsiṁha, Vāmana, Paraśurāma, Rāma, Kṛṣṇa, Buddha and Kalki are depicted.

Images of club-bearing Hanumān with folded hands are notable among the images situated at Rathurajeśvara and Lakṣmī-Nārāyaṇa at Bhoṅsalā ghāṭa. Similarly, in the image in Durgā temple at Ramnagar figures of Madhu-Kaiṭabha having sword in hand and engaged in war, are carved.

Among avatāras of Viṣṇu, Varāha has also been notable. His images are found in Mokṣeśvara temple, Durgā temple in Avaḍegrāma, Rāmnagar (Bhū-Varāha), Lakṣmī-Nārāyaṇa temple, Bhoṅsalā Ghāṭa (Narvarāha), etc. Apart from the above-mentioned, among Vaiṣṇava images, images of Viṭṭhala, Balabhadra-Subhadrā-Jagannātha, Rāma-Sītā-Lakṣmaṇa and Kṛṣṇa only two images of Viṭṭhala are known. One of those is in Lakṣmī-Nārāyaṇa temple at Bhoṅsalā Ghat and the other is placed in Kāśī Maṭha. Institution (Pañcagaṅgā Ghat). Images of Balabhadra-Subhadrā-Jagannātha can be seen in Durgā temple at Rāmnagar. Among these the image of Rāma-Sītā-Lakṣmaṇa assigned to 1582 is the oldest one which has been placed safely in Kaṅganvālī Havelī at Pañcagaṅgā Ghat.

Beside individual images, some sculptures with artistic renderings have come to light, and among those, the main scenes are holding Govardhana, trampling Kālīya, the scenes of the clothes of Draupadī being removed, deliverance of Gajendra (an elephant), Balarāma's Lomaharṣaṇa and Paraśurāma-Sahasrabāhu (*fig.* 14.3). These images can be seen in Durgā temple at Rāmnagar and Lakṣmī-Nārāyaṇa temple at Bhoṅsalā Ghat. The craftsmen of Kāśī have proved their skill by carrying out delicate carving on the stone slabs. Among Śakti icons under Vaiṣṇava image two icons assigned to ninth-tenth centuries, collected in Bharat Kala Bhavan Museum are significant, out of which one image only with the shape of Garuḍa is remaining.

Within Vaiṣṇava examples Caturviṁśati Keśava Paṭa (*fig.* 14.1) placed in Dvārakādhīśa temple at Śaṅkudhārā is especially significant from the viewpoint of characteristics of image. On the uppermost part of the plate features of face of Āditya are carved and — *kāśīkhaṇḍe keśavāya caturviṁśti mūrtayaḥ* — engraved below the figures. On this plate 24 figures in six lines (four figures each) have been engraved, sequence of the figures is given below —

Keśava, Viṣṇu, Govinda, Mādhava/Upendra, Hṛṣikeśa, Puruṣottama, Dāmodara/Pradyumna, Janārdana, Acyuta, Kṛṣṇa/Nārāyaṇa, Trivikrama, Mādhava, Madhusūdana/ Vāmana, Adhokṣaja, Nṛsiṁha, Hari/Padmanābha, Śrīdhara, Aniruddha and Sankarṣaṇa.

The Caturviṁśati Keśava Paṭa not only manifests the tradition of worship of 24 Keśavas of medieval period in Kāśī but also expresses their exposition according to ancient Śāstra.

The aforesaid description confirms that from Gupta period the present day tradition of Viṣṇu worship and image worship has been in vogue incessantly. Although, from the viewpoint of sculptural characteristics Vaiṣṇava images devoid of variety, but from the viewpoint of characteristics of style these manifest medieval regional styles. It is notable that Kāśī has been the prominent Śaiva centre but from the viewpoint of images, the number of Vaiṣṇava images is sufficiently big.

15

A Copy of "Bhāgavata Bhākhā" Illustrated in Kāśī

Rai Ananda Krishna

ART has been divided on the basis of styles but division of styles as per subjects is not rational. My topic for this write-up is Bhāgavata (Hindi Version) illustrated in local painting style in Kāśī. By good fortune this manuscript[1] composed by Phatah Singh Gvāla[2] is present in Jñāna-Pravāha collection. But I don't mean to say there was any definite painting tradition of "Vaiṣṇava style" in Kāśī, under which we get examples in this painted copy. The book is artistically illustrated. It has 423 scenes. Here we are considering only full page paintings.

This painted copy is significant for the reason that it is the oldest among the known painted scriptures of local style in Kāśī. So it deserves consideration from the viewpoint of evidence. Apart from it, there are paintings of more than one

---

1. This big sized copy is 25 × 15 cm per page in size. Apart from the empty place of margins Avadhī text is written in local Kaithī script.
2. It is the summary of *Bhāgavata Purāṇa* in *dohā* and *caupāī* genre, in mixed Avadhī language. It is believed that in later period Gosvāmī Tulasīdāsa composed *Rāmacaritamānasa* on the same model. From the viewpoint of poetry the composition is rather ordinary and the copy has been written in local Kaithī script.

style in this book. If any scholar will analyse it in future then its characteristics will be more clear.[3] Generally, it can be said that artistic style of royal court (*darabārī*) has not been used in these paintings, but these paintings represent rather middle-class bazaar style, and one can trace several *gharānā*s. The same fact is also useful in our study. It reveals that various streams of the art of painting were in practice[4] in those times. Moreover, all traditions of those streams were fixed. It is clear that those had previous history of one or two generations. It is also notable here when, in which way and how much the local art of Kāśī was influenced by the art of royal court. It has not been given desired attention nor a study has been made from the viewpoint of different styles and generations of the wall paintings. So in this text (our book in question) is significant, because at least one group of Bhāgavata's paintings connects with the traditions of these wall paintings. Because these scriptural paintings are endowed with dates, so on the basis of these dates we can determine the sequence of time and development of the aforesaid wall paintings. It is also necessary for the reason that from the period of Second World War or a little later after that the wall paintings of Kāśī have been replaced by cinema posters.

It is to be indicated that the scripture was composed during the time of Mir Rustam Ali. Our knowledge is limited to only one example about the local art of painting in those periods.

---

3. A deeper probe is necessary to analyse this work.
4. The Puṣpikā of the scripture (page 478 a/b) mentioned below— *saṁvata 1793 sāla samai nāma pūsa sudī pūrṇamāsī kaha (ko) pāṁpī (pustaka) taiyāra bhaī pāṁpī likhā nāma phatte siṁha guāla (gvāla) kā vaṅśa suta (putra) locana siṁha jamāyadāra mulājima . . . amīra rustama alī bādaśāha muhammada śāha śīnke vona iśa batanapī ārā avadha sube navāba sasādata khān, banārasī maha nāeba mīra rustama alī, paṭane sūbā alaha vīrdī khān nāeba śujā khān va ke . . . locana siṁha ke pitā vāsī ilāhābāda āge banārasī maha āya ke koniyā maha ṭike dasakhata bhora bārī rājaputa ke sākīna patnā* ।

My indication is towards the famous painting *Nīlakalama* collected in Bharat Kala Bhavan Museum. Its title is *Mīr Rustam Alī kī Holī* (Bharat Kala Bhavan collection no. 1385). We assumed it an example of the local form of the later Moghul style. From the comparative viewpoint the paintings of our copy have not been influenced with that style of royal court, instead shadow of this tradition of "Bazaar style" can be seen in the aforesaid painting of Rustam Alī. Its deep and detailed study is required.

Actual Moghul style came into existence in Kāśī from the time of Lāl Jī Musabbar.[5] From that time up to the present time in the *gharānā* of Ustād Sikkhī the same tradition is in vogue uninterruptedly with alteration and conversion in accordance with time, and we are well acquainted with it. Now it is a common question why Paradesī Ustād Lālajī Musabbar selected local (Ustād) Sikkhī (AD 1790) as his disciple ? I am sure that Ustād Sikkhī had been a traditional painter of local style and he had a reputed position. That is because Ustād Lālajī Musabbar adopted him as his disciple, who was the representative of Moghul *darabārī* painting style, the best painting style of those times. Certainly, that influence brought an ultimate change in Ustad Sikkhī's own tradition but that previous tradition can be one of those traditions which have been found in *Bhāgavata Citrāvalī*, present more than half century before this incident.

I would like to compare these *Bhāgavata* paintings with *Śabīha* of Seṭh Gavāladāsa (Bharat Kala Bhavan Collection published in Sanskrit, p. 113) These paintings are significant from the viewpoint of local artistic style in different senses and on different levels. In fact, I considered it as a typical

5. A painter came along with Śāhajāde Jabāna Bakhta, banished from royal court of Delhi. The same painter initiated Ustād Sikkhī, ancestor of Ustād Rāmaprasāda in this style. Śāhajāde Jabāna Bakhta established in Kāśī and proclaimed himself Jahādārśāha (second).

example of the last decades of the eighteenth century. We can place it under the eastern extent style of the said Rājpūt style, whose examples are being available to us one by one. Even in Bharat Kala Bhavan Museum there are several such painting series or detached paintings which have been considered from Rājasthan, etc., even these days. But now as the area of study has been extending, we have to reconsider those and place them in the area of U.P. and Bihar. Besides, there are some definite proofs, which will be considered independently at any time. Seṭh Gvāladāsa's *Śabīha* is within that extended section. He was local *seṭha* (richman) of the city, so we have to assume this *Śabīha* too an example of Benaras style. But the aforesaid *Śabīha* of Seṭha Gvāladās come under the "Mārgī" (High) art of Kāśī of those times.

It is notable that in our "*Bhāgavata*'s" paintings, at least in the paintings of its main stream, some characteristics of the aforesaid *Śabīha* are noticed as central motif. This similarity is more evident in the context of lines and colours. Their detailed analysis is possible through comparative study in future. Here I want to say that we find the big-sized paintings of "*Bhāgavata*" very close to the aforesaid *Śabīha* from some points of view. Mainly, the difference is such that the paintings belonging to "*Bhāgavata*" are not under the aforesaid "Mārgī" style. But it is also notable that for the reason of being under the style of common people they are relatively very alive and appreciating. Apart from it, no common comment has come into sight in these paintings and this confirms that this style had gained atleast two generations of experience, before having access to this level. I hope that in future the researchers will keep in mind their points in their research works of this scripture's big-sized paintings.

Comparative study of another source is also necessary here. My intention is towards a damaged copy of *Rāmacaritamānasa*, decorated with pictures and prepared by my ancestor king

Paṭanīmalla in the beginning of nineteenth century which was donated by my father to Bharat Kala Bhavan Museum. There are more than one hundred pictures of "Bālakāṇḍa" in this copy (incomplete). All these pictures belong to a different tradition from the *gharānā* of Śrī Ustād Mūlacanda, father of Ustād Rāmaprasāda. Their time frame is probably AD 1800 or just before it. Almost that was the period when Ustād Lāljī Musabbar, ancestor of Ustād Rāmaprasāda was initiating his disciple (Ustād) Sikkhī Yādav. Once I had seen a number of sketches drawn by Ustād Lāljī Musabbar (probably a painting of the same type is present in Bharat Kala Bhavan Museum). The style of that painting is totally different to the local style of Benāras. We do not have the pictures of Ustād Sikkhī or one or two generations next to him, but arriving up to Ustād Mūlacanda this tradition seems to be clear and established.

From the comparative points of view, usually there is no similarity of any sort between the pictures of *Rājā Paṭanīmalla Rāmāyaṇa* and *Jñāna-Pravāha Bhāgavata* (which belonged to about three generations before the pictures of the aforesaid *Rāmāyaṇa*). Even though, we can combine some pictures of both on the basis of some selected examples. Basically, Rājā Paṭanīmalla was not a resident of Kāśī. He settled in Kāśī in about eighteenth century AD. It is possible that he had his own painter who came to Kāśī with him. The scholars of Kala Bhavan assumed the pictures of his *Rāmāyaṇa* under Jaipur style. These pictures had also been influenced with Jaipur style. Later on I have seen some pictures of litho books influenced by this style, with the courtesy of Anjan Kumar Cakravarti. But it seems that after that imported or local styles here came to an end, but a slender influence of those is seen in the pictures of Ustād Mūlachanda, Ustād Baṭuk Prasād and (in preliminary period) Ustād Rāmaprasāda. For example it can be seen in the drawing of *Sakhiyon*.

Here we are referring to *Rāmāyaṇa* of Rājā Paṭanīmalla in a particular context. Surprising by way of exception in its wide range of pictures a few selected pages are drawn in the same local style which has been mentioned here as in the context of the pictures of the main section of *Jñāna-Pravāha Bhāgavata*. So it seems clear that Rājā Paṭanīmalla had also included some local painters in this project. But in comparison of the pictures belonging to mainstream of *Rāmāyaṇa* the local style pictures will be considered of inferior quality. So their status is parallel to "Bazaar style" similar to the picture of *Bhāgavata*. But according to it, the history of this style is almost 60 years old and if we include Gavāladāsa Sāva's *Śabīha* in it then its period has been fixed almost before 100 to 125 years. After that it had been more popular style which was found by us before 50 to 60 years mainly in the form of wall paintings. Later, this tradition almost completly vanished. It is possible that in the tradition of local Kumhār (potter) brothers we may find some remains of it drawn on the outer surface of pots as decorations during auspicious occasions.

Here one may be inclined to know the reasons for decline of that style almost after AD 1800-10. Its answer is partly based on historical evidences and rest on estimates. We know that almost from this time *gharānā* of Ustād Sikkhī was developing in Kāśī (almost AD 1800). Their art was based on Moghul style and it would have influenced local consciousness. That new consciousness was ultimately in different style. Apart from it, it is in this period the import of pictures in "company" style would have been started from Murshidabad, Patna, etc., to Kāśī. Almost in 1815 painter of this style came to Kāśī. It was naturally the expressed style which threw out our traditional style in the background.

There are some pictures of other styles too in this manuscript of *Bhāgavata* which will be discussed on some other occasion.

Appendix 1 to Chapter 15

Jalāluddīn Sāhib, a Persian scholar has given the following valuable information about this manuscript which has been included with gratitude. The title name of this scripture is *Hari Carita Bhākhā*. It was completed in Saṁvat 1587 (AD 1530). Ācārya Rāmacandra Śukla holds the opinion that probably Gosvāmī Tulasīdāsa had composed *Rāmacaritamānasa* after three generations on the same model. But from the viewpoint of poetry both the compositions have a world of difference. There is information about the book in question — *saṁvat 1793 sāla saptai nāma pūsai sudī pūrnamāsī*. It means the book was composed in 1736. In those times the province of Patna was in the region under control of Alīvardī Khān and Mīr Rustam. On the other side, Sādat Alī Khān, Nawāb of Faizabad (Avadha) and (*Bādashāh*) Muhammadsha are also mentioned. It revealed an astonishing political situation because I know that Rustam Alī had paid tributes (*khirāj*) at the royal court of Avadh. On the other hand, coming to the time of Cetasingh, tribute was paid to East India Company and that was deposited to my ancestors in Patna. East India Company took advantage of that interval of politics and on the other side Balwant Singh, the king of Benaras too. The questioned manuscript also revealed that its copyist was Phatah Singh Gāvāl (Gvāl) who lived in Koniya Muhallā of Benaras in those times, but basically he was a resident of Patna and later on dwelled in Varanasi. Phatah Singh could not be assumed commendable as copyist. As this writing is ordinary, in the same way there are small-sized ordinary pictures scattered in the pages of this scripture, but the big-sized picture is distinctive which is the topic of the write-up.

Appendix 2 to Chapter 15

The following information has been received with gratitude from Dr. Devendra Kumar Singh, the scholar of Aughaḍa literature —

Its composer was Lālaca Dāsa Halavāi of Raibareli. He composed two books — *Haricarita* in Saṁvat 1585 (AD 1528) and after two years *Bhāgavata Daśam Skandha Bhāṣā*. The famous French scholar Garsi de Tasi revealed that both the aforesaid scriptures were translated in French too (see Ramacandra Shukla, *Hindī Sāhitya Kā Itihās*, page 136).

The poet himself has given the aforesaid information mentioning his self introduction in *Bhāgavata Bhāṣā*.

Our Contributors

Prof. Ananda Krishna
Amethi Kothi, Nagava
Varanasi - 221 005

Dr. Bhanu Shankar Mehta
B - 37/67, Birdopur
Varanasi - 221 010

Prof. B.R.D. Gupta
B - 36, Kashiraj Apartment
Kamachchha
Varanasi (Uttar Pradesh)

Acharya Ganga Sharan Shastri
Sri Sadguru Kabir Mandir
Maulgadi
C - 23/5 Kabir Chaura Math
Varanasi - 221 001

Goswami Shyam Manohar Maharaj
Gopal Mandir, Chaukhamba
Varanasi - 221 001

Prof. Kamal Giri
Joint Director
Jñāna-Pravaha
Centre for Cultural Studies & Research
South of Samne Ghat
Varanasi - 221 005

Prof. M.N.P. Tiwari
Head
Dept. of History of Art
Faculty of Arts
Banaras Hindu University
Varanasi - 221 005

Dr. N.P. Joshi
CK-1/3, Pathani Tola
Bhonsla Mandir
Bhonsla Ghat
Varanasi - 221 001

Prof. Pradeep Kumar Dixit
Old H-6, Jodhpur Colony
Banaras Hindu University
Varanasi - 221 005

Dr. Pramod Giri
Giri Nagar Colony
Birdopur
Varanasi - 221 010

Dr. Pranati Ghosal
Indira Gandhi National Centre for the Arts
B 1/3 E-7, Lane No. 2
Ravindrapuri Extn.
Varanasi - 221 005

Prof. R.C. Sharma
Hon. Director/Ācārya
Jñāna-Pravaha
Centre for Cultural Studies & Research
South of Samne Ghat
Varanasi - 221 005

Prof. S.S. Sukla
B 33/71, Rohit Nagar
Naria
Varanasi - 221 005

Prof. Vasudev Singh
Dept. of Hindi
Mahatma Gandhi Kashi Vidyapeeth
Varanasi - 221 002

Prof. Vidya Nivasa Mishra
Parispanda, B-87/A-12
Bypass Road
Ravindrapuri Extn.
Varanasi - 221 005

Prof. Yugeshvar
Vedanta
C - 33/78-4
Chanua Chittupur
Varanasi - 221 002

Index

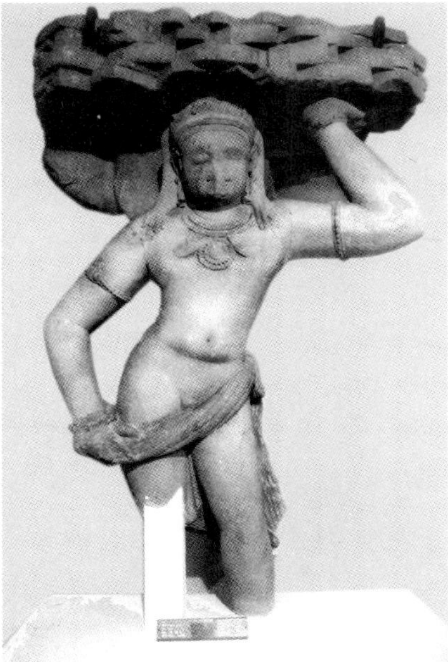

Fig. 12.1. Kṛṣṇa lifting Govardhana.

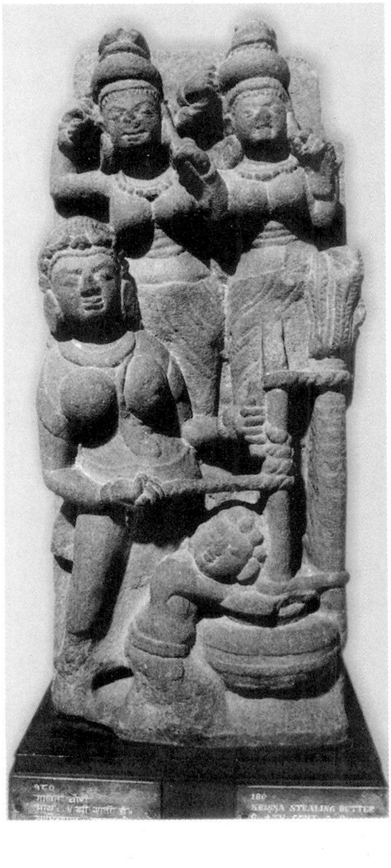

Fig. 12.2. Yaśodā charming butter.

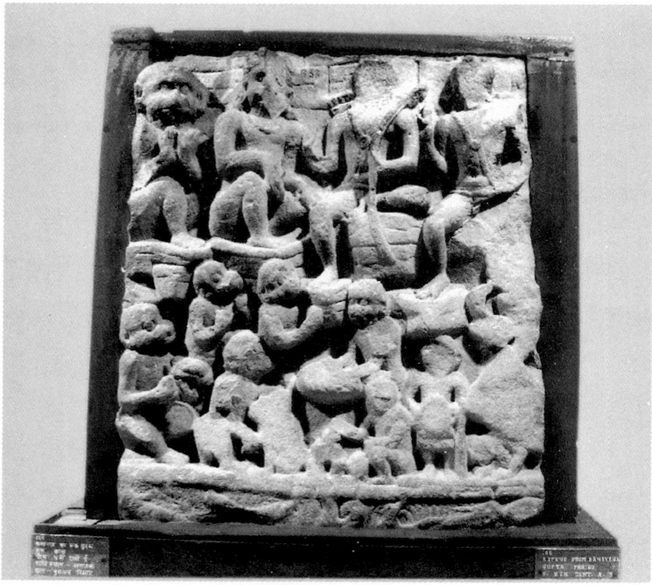

Fig. 12.3. Rāmāyaṇa scene.

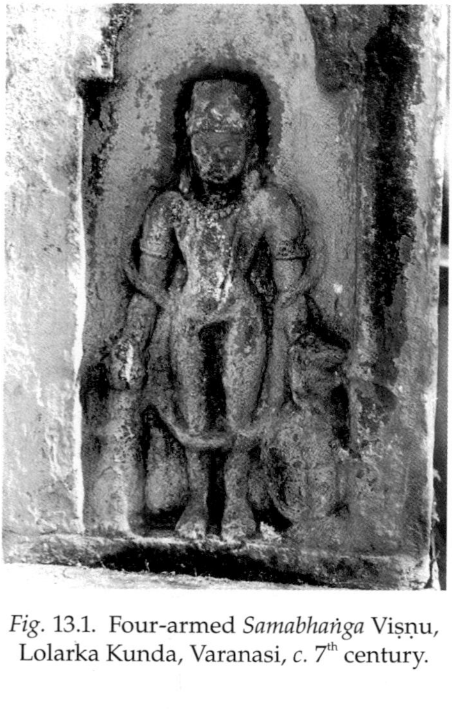

Fig. 13.1. Four-armed *Samabhaṅga* Viṣṇu, Lolarka Kunda, Varanasi, *c*. 7th century.

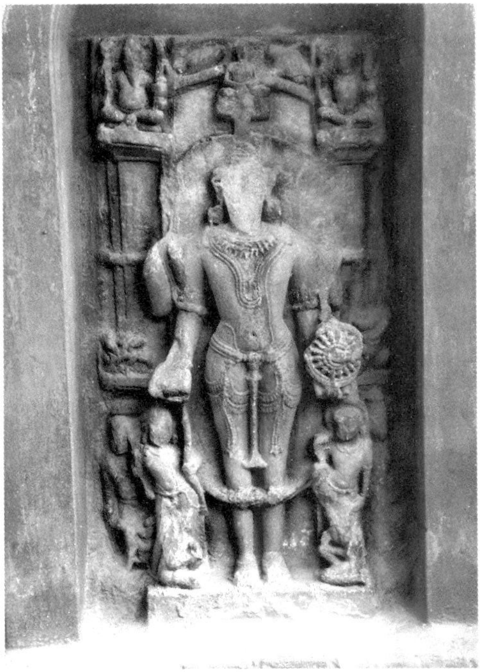

Fig. 13.2. Viṣṇu of Gāhaḍvāla style, Śuṣkeśvara Temple, Sukulpura, Varanasi, *c.* 12th century.

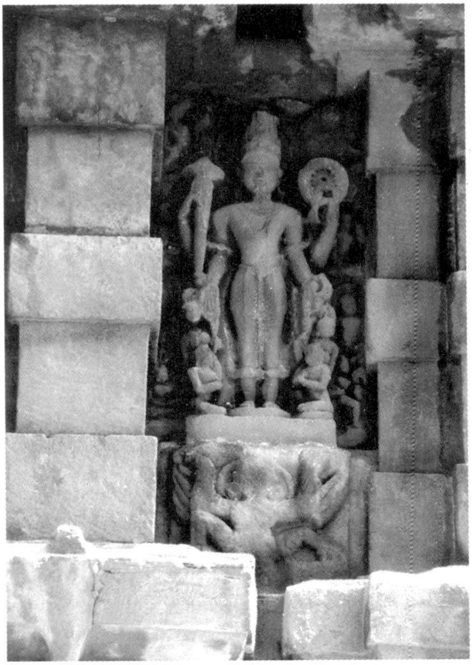

Fig. 13.3. Vāsudeva, near Kardameśvara Temple, Gāhaḍvāla style, Kandwa, Varanasi, *c.* 12th century.

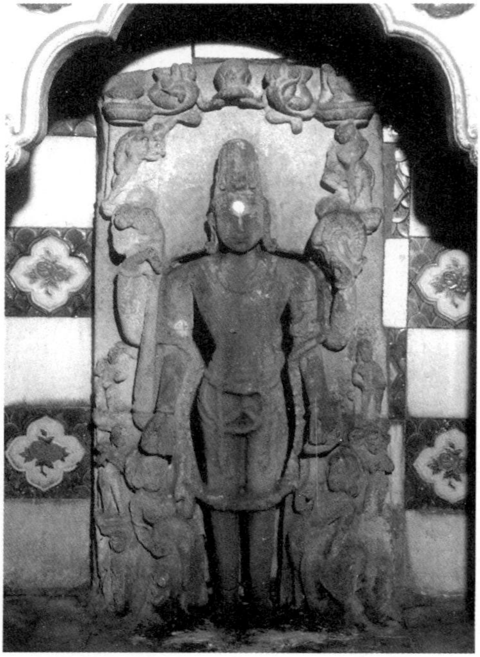

Fig. 13.4. Viṣṇu, in Trilocana Temple, Matsyodari, Varanasi, Pratihāra style, *c.* 10th century.

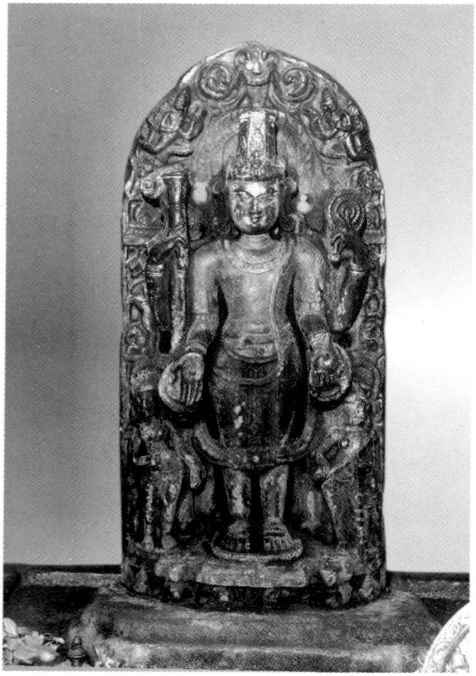

Fig. 13.5. Vāsudeva, Kasi-Matha Sansthana, Brahma Ghat, Varanasi.

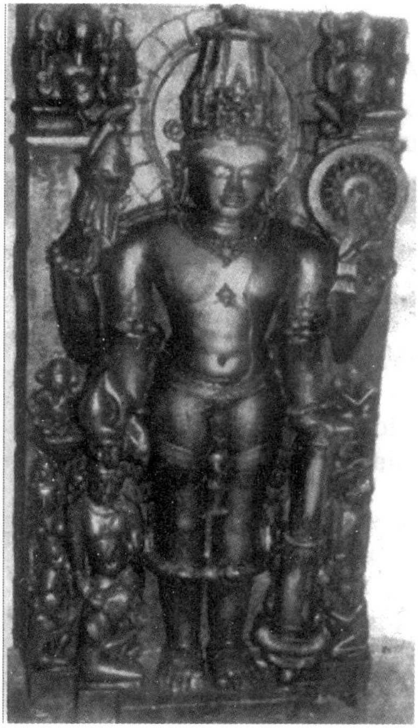

Fig. 13.6. Viṣṇu, Rāma Temple at Mansarovara Muhalla, mixed style, *c*. 10th century.

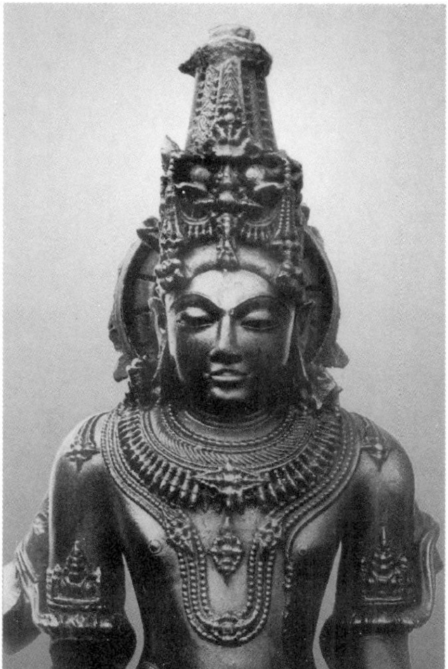

Fig. 13.7. Viṣṇu, Varanasi.

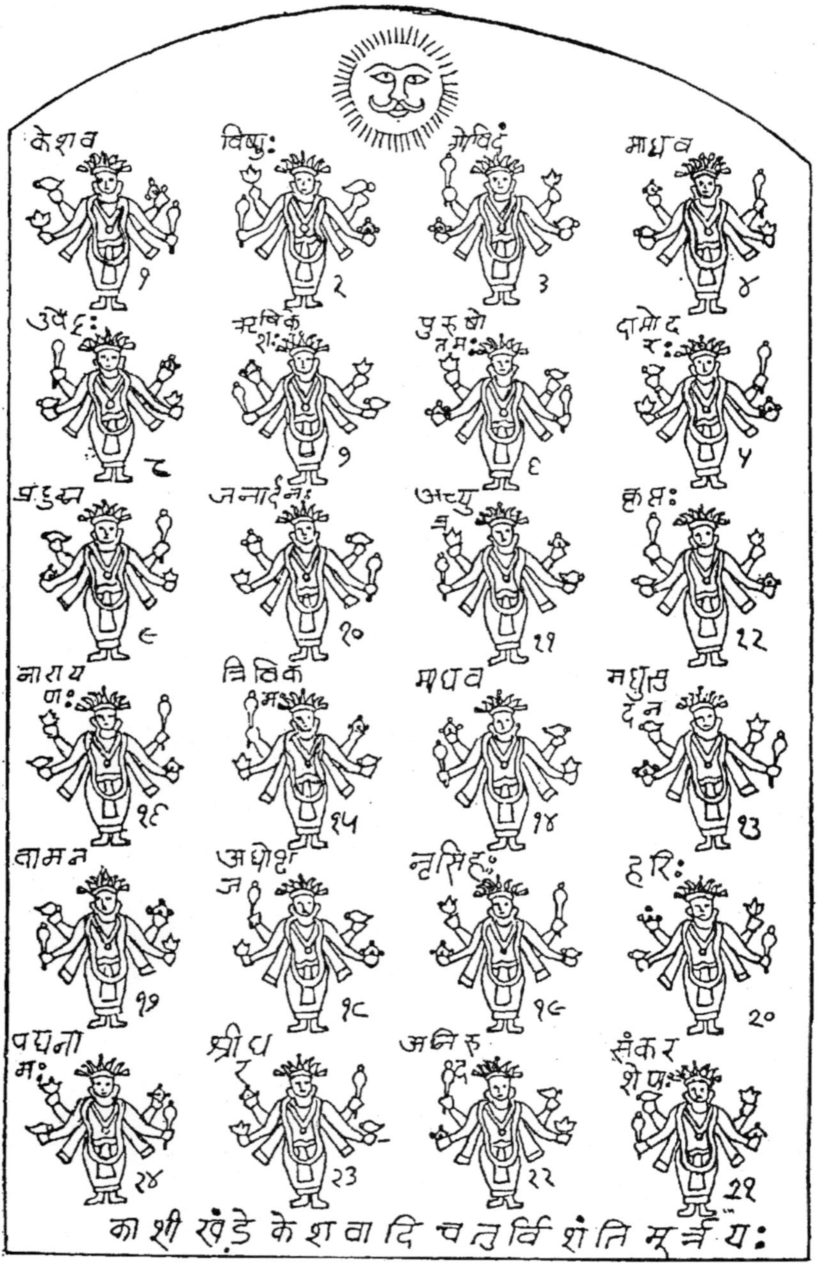

Fig. 14.1. Caturviṁśati Keśava Paṭa, Dvārikādhīśa Temple, Śankudhārā, Varanasi, 18th century (Line Drawing).

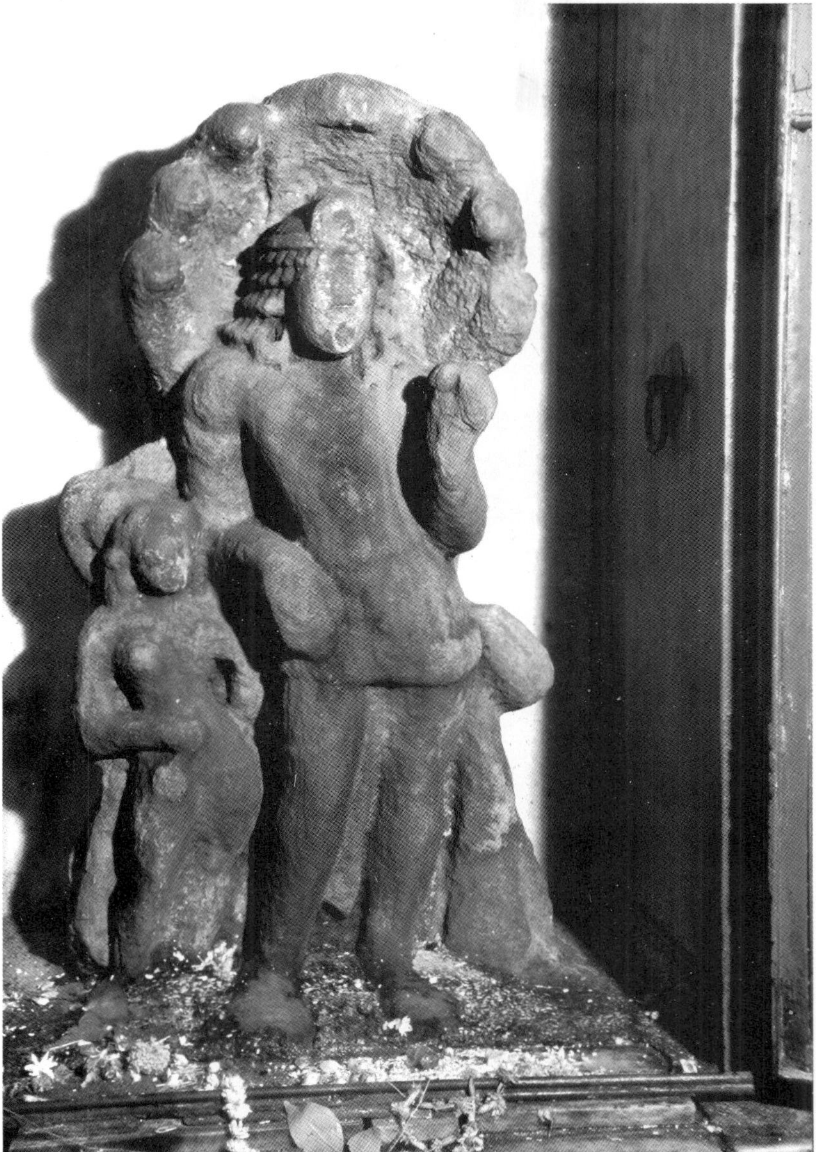

Fig. 14.2. Balarāma and Revatī, Gāyaghāṭ, Varanasi, 9th - 10th century CE.

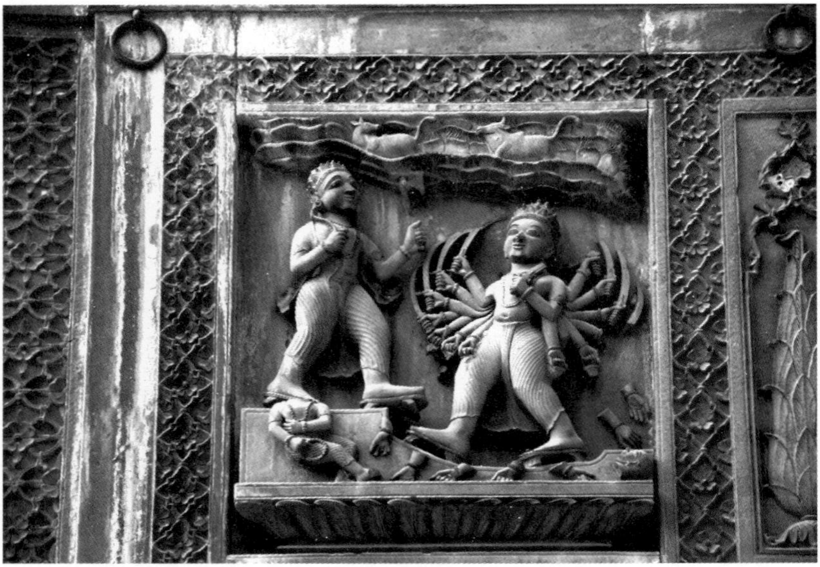

Fig. 14.3. Paraśurāma and Sahasrabāhu, Durgā Temple, Ramnagar, Varanasi, 18th century.

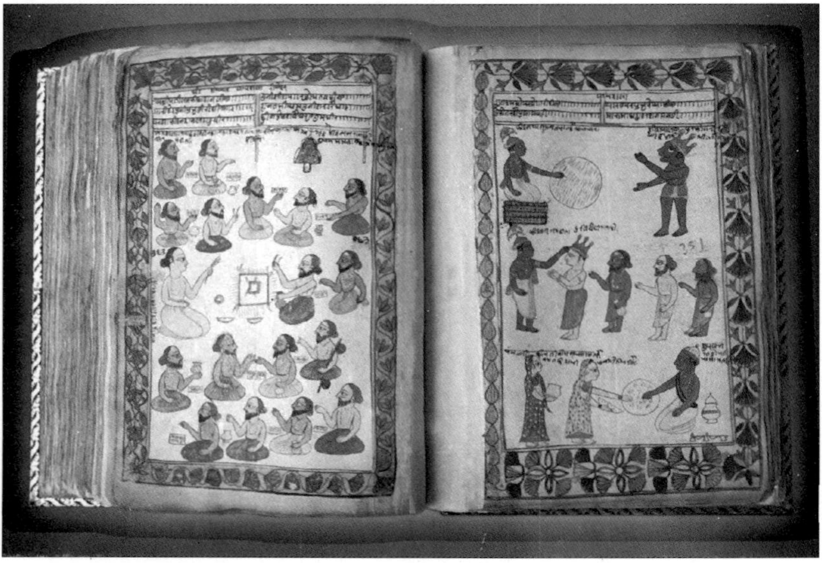

Fig. 15.1. Page from Illustrated Manuscript of *Haricarita Bhākhā*, Varanasi, CE 1736.

Fig. 15.2. Page from Illustrated Manuscript of *Haricarita Bhākhā*,Varanasi, CE 1736.